CHOOSING THE ROAD LESS TRAVELED

Finding Grace on the Path to Purpose

MYCKELLE P. WILLIAMS

Choosing the Road Less Travelled: Finding Grace On the Path to Purpose

Myckelle P. Williams

ISBN-13: 978-0615772905
ISBN-10: 0615772900

Library of Congress Control Number:

Copyright © 2013 by Myckelle P. Williams

Unless otherwise indicated, all scripture taken from the HOLY BIBLE, NEW INTERNATIONAL VERSION®. Copyright© 1973, 1978, 1984 by International Bible Society. Used by permission of Zondervan Publishing House. All rights reserved.
Frost, Robert."The Road Not Taken." The Norton Anthology of Modern Poetry. Eds. Richard Ellmann and Robert O'Clair. New York: W.W. Norton & Company, 1988. 247.
"Robert Frost." poets.org. The Academy of American Poets. 9 March 2009.

All rights reserved. No part of this book may be reproduced without written permission from the publisher, except by a reviewer who may quote brief passages in a review; nor may any part of this book be reproduced, stored in a retrieval system or transmitted in any form or other without written permission from the publisher.

This book is manufactured in the United States of America.

Editor: Janet Schwind
Cover Design: idrewdesign

Note: *Some names have been changed to protect the privacy of the people in this book.

Choosing the Road Less Traveled: Finding Grace on the Path to Purpose
Myckelle P. Williams
Based on the poem *The Road Not Taken* by Robert Frost
MPowerment Worldwide, LLC
PO Box 431
Collierville, TN 38027
www.mpowermentww.org

*This Book is dedicated to the lost, wounded, and broken woman who
stands at a crossroads in her own life.
Know that as you face your choices,
you are not alone, and that the creator of the Universe
still sees, loves, and
pursues you with an unfailing love....
Choose God. Choose Life.
~ Deuteronomy 30:19*

For the Reader….

"For I know the plans I have for you," declares the LORD, *"plans to prosper you and not to harm you, plans to give you hope and a future."*~ Jeremiah 29:11

When God creates us, he has a Vision in mind. As Jeremiah 29:11 states, he has PLANS for us. He sees in us what we fail to see in ourselves. He sees what we are going to be, not what we are. And everything He does during our upbringing is for the purpose of growing us into what we are meant to be. The end result is what God sees from the time he placed us in our mother's womb. And all of the talents, gifts and abilities that he placed in us are there to help accomplish the **Purpose** that He has for our lives. Eventually, it is intended to prosper us, give us hope, and a future.
This book is my own unique journey of a road less travelled—but perhaps, one that is not so uncommon as I at one time believed. I share how I survived a teenage pregnancy, and overcame generational dysfunction, to raise a more stable next generation.

Using Robert Frost's poem as a foundation, I will attempt to lead you, the reader, on a journey of self-discovery, revealing how the choices I made impacted my life—lessons I hope my readers can learn from, and develop hope in. You may feel that you have been previously stuck in a cycle that can't be broken, but my story proves it is possible to pull off the dead weeds from your past, and regrow new roots for the future…just by making different choices in life than those of the generations before you.
I pray that reading this book blesses you as much as it blessed me to write it.

It is important in your own life that you seek to learn and understand your purpose, and then begin to walk in it, and pursue it with an unwavering faith, focusing on the end result! It's what you were made for…wasn't it?! Don't look at who and what you are *now*, and allow the enemy to condemn you for not getting there yet, because **his job** is to Deceive, Discourage, Distract, and Disrupt the purpose that God has for your life. Know that as long as you are still breathing, it's never too late to re-focus, change behaviors, and choose a different path. God is still working in, on, and through you!

Remind yourself daily that you are God's Purposed Creation, made with a vision, valuable and unique. Despite the problems you've faced in life, you are a beautiful, powerful, valuable creation of God. Yes, you! You can live a happy, healthy life - and it begins with renewing your heart and mind. There are certain things that only YOU can do, certain people that only YOU can reach. Maybe, like me, you will be able to one day look back over your life and see those times that God clearly had a plan and things came together for your good the way they were supposed to. Or maybe you are still seeking to find answers. Either way, God doesn't want to keep your purpose from you. He wants you to get on the path that He laid out for you, because it is only there, within His will, that you will find true fulfillment, peace, and blessings that await you.

Now the question is: when will you decide that it's time to step out and become who you were *born* to be?

–Myckelle P. Williams

ACKNOWLEDGEMENTS

Humble Thanks

Heartbeat Ministries, and Crisis Pregnancy Center Volunteers everywhere who don't know me, but changed my life for the better: Never give up on your fight to save the unborn, and know that you are making a difference, even when it sometimes feels like a lost cause.

Pastor Chuck Smith, Greg Laurie, and the Entire Calvary Chapel Costa Mesa/Riverside Family, your ministry was a blessing to me, and I became a woman through the uncompromising Word that you taught there. It was an honor to be a member of your congregation.

My parents, Addreinne and Michael, thank you both for lessons learned, good and painful, that helped to make me who I am today. You both did the best that you could, and I love you both and pray that God will continue to bless each of you, and bring you into the full knowledge of who He is.

Miss Cherry White, wherever you are, I pray hundredfold blessing on your life and family. Thank you for loving those children and imparting Jesus into them. Because of the seed that you planted, this story can be told.

Deborah Durham, Roz Heaton, Donna and Corrine, my "Hope Center Crew," the original "beautiful ladies of grace" who challenged and inspired me to continue to love and pray for the seemingly unlovable, thank you for your hours of hard work and determination. It is not in vain! Hope to see you again one day.

World Changers Church International, and Dr. Creflo and Taffi Dollar who taught me how to live blessed and prosperous, and gave me a part of a ministry that operated in excellence, causing me to raise my own standards, and realize that I am "blessed to be a blessing."

Marriage ministry leaders Ray and Lisa Smith, a beautiful couple who overcame so much to impart God's Word into our lives and the lives of other couples, you two are powerful! God bless your family, and continue to make a mark that can't be erased.

My covenant partners Miles, Vanessa, Dwight, Eleanor, I love you all dearly, and pray that we finish the purpose that God had when he bound us together in Covenant. Thank you for your love, prayers, and encouragement, and for giving me the motivation to go for my dreams.

Sheila and Julian Sinegal who showed me what unconditional love is. The love and dedication that you share for each other and your children consistently inspired me, and the laughs that we shared will never be forgotten. Julian, you are such a pillar of strength within your family…keep focusing on Him, and He will uplift you to where you need to be.

Shelia Perales, who rescued and comforted me so many times when I ran away from home; loving, encouraging, and listening to all of my complaints and heartaches; telling me that I was destined for great things. Being the best friend since the age of twelve, you never judged me, and simply were there when I needed you. I love you, girl. You are so special…and beautiful, inside and out.

To the lost and confused women/clients who reminded me of me as a young, frightened girl, you are not alone. God loves you and fights daily for you in the spiritual realm. Trust in Him.

The Nu Lyfe in Christ Crew #TeamJesus...the best crew of young people ever, on fire for Christ and make me proud of you every day. Thank you for your hard work and dedication to His calling.

Katrina Smith, my partner, friend, and sister in B.L.O.G, for encouraging me to tell my stories by the example you set in Butterfly Ministries. You have grown so much in even this past year, and I can't tell you what you do to encourage me. Thank you for stretching, challenging, and encouraging me to be all that I can be in Christ, and your wise words and beautiful writing that push me to get better as well.

To all the B.L.O.G. Magazine™ ladies...our fabulous editors Tameka, Kairis, Kischa, and Jessica and our amazing team of writers, you never fail to inspire me with your tireless dedication to empowering, inspiring and enlightening! Also my new sisters at BLOGTalk Live! Josette, Tanya, and Chantelle. I look forward to growing in Christ with you all. You are indeed Beautiful Ladies of Grace!

Thank you also to the people who contributed to the effort that it took to get this book published, and patiently answered all of my questions with such grace and compassion. You also inspired me to learn more: Dave from Fiverr, Janet Schwind, Angela Ardis, Cindy Lumpkin, and the Trinity Publishing group.

My children, Gerald, Ashley, Briana, Adrien, Kayla and Lauren. You are my eternal heartbeats. Without you, I would not be the woman I am today. You motivated me to do, grow, and be better every day. Your laughter, tears, fights, and make-ups were still music to my soul, and I love you each with everything inside of me. You are not just my children: You are my best friends…this is your story as much as mine. May you continue to keep God first unto the next generations after us, and continue in the legacy of God's love started in me, fanning the flame among his chosen ones.

My husband, Gerald, you have loved me since I was a gawky teen, and encouraged me to tell my story because it needed to be told, and pushed me to write daily until I got it done. Thank you so much for your love, persistence, and support. You are there when I need you, and I thank God for bringing you into my life and sharing my children with me. You are a wonderful father and a supportive husband, and thank you for seeing in me what I sometimes don't see in myself. To twenty more years together, even better than the first.

Karen and David Hanson, words can **never** express my love for you, and my eternal gratitude for the lessons and love that you imparted into me. You are my inspiration of what I still try and often fail to emulate. Thank you for taking a chance on me, and having a wonderful sense of humor during it all. I pray for you daily, and can't wait to one day see you again.

My Heavenly Father above, there aren't many words that I can say to express how awed I am of the fact that You loved me before I even knew You did. Despite my many flaws and imperfections, You have pursued me and given me life and purpose before my birth, and I am truly humbled by that. Forgive those times that I haven't appreciate the lessons and correction, and strayed from you. Continue to mold, shape, and create in me a clean heart after You. I love you, Father, more each day, and thank You for all of my blessings. I am still amazed by what You are doing in and through me, and I ask that You only continue to use me as a willing vessel to share Your Word. It is only through Your will that this book is even possible.

Amazing Grace…

CONTENTS

INTRODUCTION 15
PROLOGUE 17
PART 1: THE CHOICE 21
CHAPTER 1: Nowhere to Run 22
CHAPTER 2: Hidden Away 36
CHAPTER 3: Options 49
CHAPTER 4: Fork in the Road 58
PART 2: A NEW LIFE 65
CHAPTER 5: The Hansons 66
CHAPTER 6: From Rebellion to Love 80
CHAPTER 7: Born Again 93
CHAPTER 8: A Special Surprise 100
PART 3: A COVENANT DECISION 105
CHAPTER 9: A New Creation! 106
CHAPTER 10: The Birth 113
CHAPTER 11: Homecoming 121
CHAPTER 12: Wedding Bells 130
CHAPTER 13: Goodbyes 137
PART 4: LAYING FOUNDATIONS 141
CHAPTER 14: The Newlywed Life 142
CHAPTER 15: A Call to Leave 147
CHAPTER 16: Full Circle 151
CHAPTER 17: Endings and Beginnings 159
Epilogue 164

INTRODUCTION

Myckelle.

Strange name, strange spelling. Far too many extra consonants. For the major part of my life, my name was a source of embarrassment and shame. Teachers could never pronounce it, and I was always having to correct someone who killed the pronunciation of it. People laughed at and even sometimes teased me over it. I have never found anyone who could randomly guess how to spell it correctly. Growing up, I didn't understand why my parents even chose the name. Now, as an adult, however, I can appreciate that my name is different. What once was a source of embarrassment is now a badge of honor. I am unique…and wonderfully and fearfully made, I later discovered. My life story is as special as my name.

I am a pioneer within my family. Not the kind who wears a bonnet and shawl and travels the open country in a covered wagon, like Laura Ingalls Wilder. More like the character in my favorite Robert Frost poem, *The Road Not Taken*. For me, there came a crucial point in my life where I faced a major crossroads and had to make a decision on a life path in which to travel. I was literally at a fork in the road, as we all sometimes confront while traveling life's journey. By choosing to take a direction different from the generations before me, I became within my own family a person of many "firsts": The first to live a drug free, family-oriented life. The first to break the cycle of promiscuity and abuse. The first to become a Christian, living a life in service to God and others. It was not easy, and along the way I made and still continue to make plenty of mistakes. But like other pioneers before me, I had to forge my own path, and learn through trial and error. The lessons that we learn along the journey, we can pass on to a future generation, to make their path a little easier to travel the next time around.

Many of us don't think it's possible, but any of us can forge a new path in our own family, breaking the strongholds and generational patterns, or "curses," that were there before we came along. Sometimes it takes just one person willing to be a pioneer and decide they want something different than what they saw growing up. My hopes are that as you read my story, you too will be inspired to create new traditions and generational patterns in your own family as well as breaking old strongholds and ties that threaten to keep you and your children from the purpose that God intended.

You can also be like Abraham, going out from among the family and stepping into a *"new thing" to which God calls us* (Isaiah 43:19). Hindsight is always 20/20. Looking back, I realize that what I thought was a lonely childhood and a difficult adolescence, was actually preparation for my destiny.

I took the road less traveled by ... and that has made all the difference.

PROLOGUE

Before I formed you in the womb, I knew you. Before you were born, I set you apart for my holy purpose...I appointed you to be a prophet to the nations.
~Jeremiah 1:5

"I'd like to make an appointment...for an abortion."

Desperation and shame filled my voice, and I hoped the lady on the other end didn't know me or my parents.

"How many weeks are you? When was your last period?" The lady on the other end asks, seemingly not surprised, sounding more annoyed than anything else.

I gave her the dates she requested, asking "How much will that cost?" Annoyed sigh. "You are fourteen-and-a-half weeks. Well, the process will be much longer because you are further along, but it will be $375 total."

"Do you take Medicaid?"

"Yes."

"When can I come in?

"Tuesday at 8 a.m.

"Do I need to bring anything?"

"Just your money, or Medicaid card, proof of pregnancy. And a ride home."

I hung up and looked at my boyfriend. How were we going to afford that? We could barely afford to take care of our eleven month old son, the child I had had less than a year ago at age seventeen. "It's cool." He told me. "My sister has Medicaid. We can use her card. You just use her name and info."

"Do you think she would let me?" I wasn't sure that I could even pull that off at my age. His sister was in her twenties and looked much older than I.

"I already asked her. She said okay."
Wow, I thought. He obviously was already thinking one step ahead.

So it was all set. I had an appointment to get rid of my "problem." I didn't want my family to find out that, once again, I had messed up my life. Although we had used condoms this time around, it seemed I would be looked at again as just a "screw-up."

I would be eighteen years old with two children. That seemed crazy. Many women in our family, including my mother, had had multiple abortions with no problems. So it must not be that bad, I thought. Right?

It's just the termination of a pregnancy. Removal of unwanted tissue. Kind of like extracting a bad tooth or removing a mole...I tried hard to convince myself of this.

Besides, I was supposed to be the smart one, the kid who was supposed to DO SOMETHING with her life. So far all I felt I had accomplished was to have one baby, and struggle as a teen mother to graduate high school.

The waves of nausea washed over me, reminding me of my ever-impending condition.

I knew I couldn't put it off any longer. Soon I would start to show. I just wanted it to be over as quickly as possible. In my mind, abortion was the best and quickest way out of this "mess."

PART 1

THE CHOICE

Two roads diverged in a yellow wood,
And sorry I could not travel both
And be one traveler, long I stood
And looked down one as far as I could
To where it bent in the undergrowth

CHAPTER 1

Nowhere to Run

LIFE IS A SERIES OF CHOICES. Everyone starts off born with a "blank slate," having unlimited potential, and the ability to be and do many things. At our foundation, God starts each of us off with three special gifts. First, a purpose and a plan for our lives that initially we are unaware of. He then places within us certain talents and abilities that enable us to fulfill that purpose. Last, He gives us something very interesting, something to prevent us from feeling as if we are mindless robots walking around forced to do what He wants us to do—it's called *free will*. This free will allows us the choice to serve Him or rebel against Him, to believe in Him or deny Him, to obey Him, or disobey Him, to love Him, or some other god, or no God at all.

From the very first human being, God never denied us our ability to make these choices. Many people say that the tree of Knowledge of Good and Evil should never have been planted in the first place, and that God was tempting people by doing that, because He knew what would happen. Others say that had the tree not been there, we could have just lived forever with God in paradise and there would have been no problem. They use this as a reason why we are destined to continue to fall short of His will. However, I look at it differently. In any relationship, if you are forced to obey and have no other options, it's not really your *will*. I mean, seriously, think about it: If I was brought to a desert island as a child by a guy who wanted to be with me, and raised with no other men around (sort of a Blue Lagoon experience), of course it would be easy to eventually love him. But if he never let me leave, and told me I *had* to be with him for the rest of my life and love him, because if he let me off the island he knows that I'd one day cheat on him, not only would I be offended, but I would resent him as being insecure and controlling, and for not allowing me to find this out for myself. Experiencing other people and having options, yet still choosing to be with that person would show me (and him) that my choice is *willing*. And when he trusts me enough to make a good or bad decision, I feel as if I want to do the right thing to please him. Bottom line, if I choose to stay, despite our issues and obstacles, then he really knows that I truly love him.

So I would like to submit to you that God is *pro-choice*. It may sound funny, but it's true. God says clearly in Deuteronomy 30:19: *This day I call heaven and earth as witnesses against you that I have set before your life and death, blessings and curses. Now choose life…so that you and your children may live.*

God gives us the choice to choose what we want to do with our hearts, lives, and families. He even is kind enough to "recommend" a choice: Life. But He neither forces that choice upon us nor manipulates our will into selecting that path. He simply allows us the room to decide whether or not we will truly love and obey Him. Therefore, when things go wrong in our lives as a result of making the wrong choices, we cannot turn around and blame God, our parents, or anyone else as Adam and Eve did. We must take responsibility for our own choices because we all have them, even today, in every area of our lives. And as He reminds us in the above verse, what we do with that choice will determine not only our future, but the future of our children and their children. In other words, He is saying "Choose wisely!" God didn't place the tree in the garden to "trap" or "trip up" Adam; he did it to offer a choice to love and to be obedient. That is an act of unselfish love by an unselfish God. If we made the wrong decision, we can't blame Him for the temptation just because we couldn't control ourselves.

When tempted, no one should say, "God is tempting me." For God cannot be tempted by evil, nor does he tempt anyone; but each one is tempted when, by his own evil desire, he is dragged away and enticed (James1:13-14).

~~~~~~~~

Like the traveler in my favorite Robert Frost poem, I once stood on the edge of a major life-changing decision as an eighteen-year-old teenager, pregnant with my second child. In my mind, another baby would really hinder my life and my future. I tried to look down the road as far as I could and all I saw was struggle. I felt as if my choices were limited: I could either have my education, and promise for a future…or be a teen mom on welfare. I didn't want to raise another child in chaos and confusion, without it having married parents, like I was raised. What we learn from our parents growing up usually manifests itself in one of two ways: we either become exactly like them, or we do the opposite than they did.

My childhood was rather unstable to say the least. Both of my parents were runaways who came from abusive situations. My mother had been a teen mother herself, having me at eighteen. I was born in 1973, the year abortion became legal. The fact that my mother did not abort me is mind-blowing, considering that I am the only child she didn't abort. The others after me weren't so fortunate. My mother was beautiful, funny, and smart, extremely independent, not really meant for a domestic life. She met my dad at seventeen. They were already both living on their own, and they moved into a rental house together. They never married. They were passionate, both headstrong, and by the time I was a year and a half, they were already split up so I never remember them being a couple.

My mother decided after having me that she had a decision to make between being a wife, and mother, or making it on her own, and in her mind, children and family did not equal success; she considered it being trapped into failure. She stood on the edge of a decision—of a marriage and family—and chose instead to change her destiny and leave my father at the altar, and start over with nothing.

After that, my parents took two separate life paths, and became as different as night and day. Mom got a great job as a sales rep at Xerox and began a life in corporate America. She was brilliant and financially savvy, so she was able to buy her first house at twenty-three years old.

I never saw her struggle. She always had an expensive car, beautiful things, nice furniture, and lovely homes. She dated men with lots of money and power, went on lavish trips, and always had beautiful clothes and jewelry. Her friends were much older, well spoken, the black elite who listened to jazz music and went to clubs several nights a week. She was living the life. Unfortunately, this lifestyle left little room for parenting. I was left alone a lot, starting at age six.

My father was handsome, strong, and comedic. He was dark skinned with reddish curly hair, hazel-grey eyes, and a cleft chin like John Travolta. Women *loved* him, chased him, fought over him, and he loved them too... so much so that he eventually became a pimp and had them in constant flow. He was a drug dealer most of my life, and I would often see suitcases full of money in his possession. Parties were constant throughout my childhood. My parents, although in love as teens, did not get along while I was growing up. They both were bitter from the way things ended between them. In my mind, my mother seemed to almost hate him, and constantly talked about him and his "ghetto" lifestyle. She would call him only when she had a violent fight with a boyfriend (which was often), and he would come over and beat the guy senseless. I admired his strength and saw him as a hero. I stayed with Mom until age eight and would visit Dad often, or rather, whenever my mother didn't get mad at him and forbid it. I hated the back and forth moving, the fights I witnessed, the constant switching of partners that I watched them both do.

I never felt a sense of stability and normalcy growing up, and so I desperately wanted that one day for myself in the form of my own real family. But I didn't really see a stable family as an example, unless it was on television. My dad was once so in love with my mother, and so crushed by her abandonment at the altar that from what I saw, he never trusted, was loyal to, or respected another woman again. When I visited my dad at his house, the closest we came to a "nuclear family" was that he got a girlfriend pregnant twice and had two children with her. So I considered her my stepmother, although they never married either.

Unfortunately, he was always cheating with other women during their twelve-year relationship, and brought us kids along to meet and hang around these other women, who were oftentimes prostitutes and models. At the time, I saw nothing negative in this. I loved my stepmother, but I liked the other women, too. I just thought that they were all a fun bunch. They all freely did drugs, and there was always music blaring, laughter, and dancing throughout the house. My little brother and I were often deejays at their parties (funny, he is a deejay still to this day). In my dad's neighborhood, people came and went without knocking. You could literally walk into your neighbor's apartment, open their fridge, and get their milk with no problem. Everyone in that complex was friends, and they had lots of children, so I had many new buddies to play with.

At Dad's house, there were constant adult parties where folks ended up drunk or high and in their underwear, and the beautiful strippers were really sweet to me and took me under their wings and taught me things, like how to play cards, and I even learned the recipe to make crack from cocaine. It sounds bizarre, but this was in the early 1970s, just after the Sexual Revolution had taken place, so sex and drugs were plentiful and considered "cool." It was fun times to me, and I actually preferred my dad's house over my mother's, because at least he spent quality time with me. In my young, impressionable mind, my dad was Superman and could do no wrong. He was charming, funny, and crazily adventurous, especially when high. He would stand on rooftops and claim to be Jesus, and sing and joke as he drove us through the city in a car with no brakes. Being in his presence was always an adrenaline rush. He also loved to sing, and had a great voice. There was always music and loud singing going on at all times in his home. He had visions of being a stand-up comedian as well, and would constantly tell jokes that kept everyone in tears. He is the funniest person I know, and is how we all developed our senses of humor. He says that his mother was comedic as well. To this day, my dad will call and tell me to write down his latest joke...we often laugh till we cry.

These things to me outweighed the fact that he also engaged in criminal activity, because to me, he was just "Daddy."

Regardless of my mother and dad's relationship with each other and the lifestyle he led, I can honestly say that he was a good and loving parent to me and his other children, when we were young. He never hit us, was affectionate, and a constant teacher. He wanted us to know about school things as well as "street life." He wanted kids who were smart in all ways. When I was about three, he taught me what nouns, verbs, and superlatives were, and constantly quizzed me in front of crowds. We had a running script. He would teach me Spanish words and multiplication and division tables long before I learned them in school. He loved education and believed in being "self-taught." He watched hours of Discovery Channel, History Channel, and read encyclopedias for knowledge.

Many people have prejudices about what people with criminal histories are like, but many of them are extremely brilliant people. My father was a master at debate, and because he was well-read and well-spoken, he managed to speak and congregate with some wealthy people. The problem was the presence of drugs in this environment—both the drugs and the money to be made from them were so addictive that it also influenced behaviors in other ways, turning many a smart man down a dark path. But, there was nothing my dad did or anywhere he went that he didn't take my younger brother and me, nothing we didn't see or know about. My father laughed and joked with all of the neighborhood kids and taught us all to dance and play games in the streets until late in the night. He allowed us to taste alcohol and try cigarettes, which we all decided we hated. He was very strong and muscular, and many people were afraid of him. I saw him beat several huge men unconscious. He was fearless.

A couple of times when grown men got too "sweet" with me, my dad would choke them and put them in their place, telling them not to even look at his daughter. I'd seen grown men begging him on their knees for mercy.

He never had to spank us because one yell at us kept us in check. If I felt that I had disappointed him for any reason, I would burst into tears because I wanted to please him, plus I feared him with a deep respect for who he was in our town.

Interestingly enough, none of my dad's kids became involved in a negative lifestyle. We never did drugs, drank, or participated in criminal activity. Besides my dad, none of us were incarcerated or got in trouble. So, in a way, he had a big influence on us. We looked at his lifestyle as a book of "What Not to Do" and took different paths. This is not to endorse his lifestyle, but it goes to show that this isn't always a predictor of how children will turn out. There were many children I saw in school who were the daughters and sons of pastors, who acted much worse than (and used the same language and behaviors of) many of the pimps and hustlers I'd seen growing up. And on the flip side, there were many sons and daughters of crack heads who I saw struggling to get to school and be educated, even when they had to walk or make a way there, with their parents passed out high.

I enjoyed my relationships with the women my father dated—they were all beautiful, smart, and hilariously funny. But through his toxic relationships with them, my dad taught me some lessons of great value about men and their ways. He and all his player friends would sit me down and "school" me on what they did to manipulate women. It sounds almost shocking, but they did this out of a paternal love for me, as they all considered me a second daughter and didn't want me caught up in being a victim like the women they dealt with. They would take me in their rooms and show me the hidden video cameras they used to secretly videotape sex acts; you could not see the cameras hidden in places like tissue boxes! Then they would take me back into the den where the picture on the seventy-two-inch big-screen TV would show the entire "show" from there, unknown to the poor women, in full view of every guest in the home—usually a house full of men, laughing and watching.

They were creative indeed. I watched how they would call their "main" girlfriend on the phone and talk to her, saying they were going to bed early and they love her, even when the "side" girlfriend was sitting right there listening and watching. These men held nothing back from me. I was amazed, and pitied these poor women, who trusted and loved these men so much. Some of the men were married, and I would see them with their wives and children, and then again with their mistresses and children. One of my dad's friends was a millionaire; he had three sons with his wife…and three daughters with his mistresses. His wife was so upset that they couldn't have a girl, but everyone else knew he was having girls everywhere else in town! All I could do was absorb everything. It was more complex than any reality show on TV today.

Some of the men were illiterate, and I would read to them, which they loved. I met and formed relationships with their women, who would treat me like their little personal psychiatrist, telling me all their problems and detailing their heartbreak as I listened. As a child, I rarely hung out with other children. Adults loved having me around and talked to me like I was one of them. If one of them was cheating with the other one, they told me. If they had herpes or abortions, they told me. I have no idea why they felt so comfortable confiding with a child, but I suppose I was a good listener. I never told anyone's secrets and I never participated in gossip, so I think they felt they could trust me. To this day, I have knowledge of a very well-known celebrity today who THINKS his son is his, but the mother of the son confided in me that he is really not, yet he pays for and has claimed this child as his own to this very day. Looking back, with all that I learned, I developed knowledge of people and behaviors, which is possibly why I am still interested in psychology as a course of study. I had a personal, hands-on *Think Like a Man* and *He's Not That Into You* childhood education. The men were handsome, and some had money, but I was taught what to look for and how to avoid a player. Aside from the crime and drug use, I do think every father needs to teach his daughter those "man lessons". He could save her a lot of heartache and make her wise at an early age, so that she doesn't become a victim to today's "wolves in sheep's clothing." When little girls are overly sheltered, they develop a trust in some people that they shouldn't, and many times do not understand the ways of the conniving men who have an ulterior motive, which causes pain and betrayal like it did for so many of the beautiful ladies I encountered. Through my lessons, I was able to avoid many of those games, because I saw them coming in advance.

My mother and her friends, on the other hand, were quite different than my dad and his in many ways, but alike in others. My mom was much more serious, very proper, and elite. She always reminded me of a black Erica Kane. She was beautiful and desirable, a light skinned woman with fluffy reddish-blonde Farrah Fawcett hair and a curvy physique, full lips, a huge smile, and freckles. I watched many men lust for her openly. She only dated older rich men, none of whom were particularly interesting or appealing to me. Many of them looked like a grandfather type, and in retrospect, I think my mother gravitated toward older men because she missed having her father in her life. Her parents divorced before she was in her teens, and she tried to stay in communication with her father, whom she loved greatly. Her mother was white, and he was African American, and her connection to her black roots. However, he moved on after the divorce, and married another woman, having two more children (one of whom is only two weeks older than I am). My mother called him and asked to meet with him one day, at which time he promptly told her, "Look, I have a new family now. Please do not *ever* call me again." My mother was crushed, and from that day on claimed to have "abandonment issues" (her words). She sought attention from men, and fought to keep them in her life. One love interest in particular was a married man. His wife would show up at our house and beg my mother to leave her husband alone. This married man, Stan*, also had a small son named Karl, less than a year old, which he would bring over to play with me while Stan went in the room for hours with my mother. I enjoyed younger children, and considered little Karl like a little brother to me. We would go on camping trips to Stan and his wife's cabin in the mountains of Big Bear, and Stan was a frequent visitor to our home. He fixed things at our house, helped us move, and ate dinner with us often. My mother was crazy about him.

Such an odd little family…even at age six, I knew he was married and decided I didn't like him because of it. By dealing with my fathers married cheating friends, I knew that married men did not tend to respect the women they cheated with. That was a problem to me, and also the fact that he always looked at my mother with pure lust in his eyes. It bothered me to see any man treating my mother like a piece of meat. I just knew in my heart that this was wrong and that he needed to be with his wife and leave my mother alone (although I never said it out loud). My mother, however, adored him and had no idea that I knew he was married. They secretively spelled words around me, even though I could read full books, and knew exactly what they were saying. Mom worked hard to impress him and keep him coming around, often dressing in very revealing clothes whenever he came over. It irritated me. You never want to see your mother as a sexual person in any way. I could accept that in my dad, because he was a man, but not her. I would be jealous of and rude to her boyfriends. My mother tried her best to hide her sex life from me, but several times I accidentally walked in on her, and it made me angry, and her embarrassed.

My mother had a group of girlfriends who were older, fun, and hilarious. They went to the clubs three days a week, and I would watch them get ready in their cute, tight, revealing dresses and talk about the latest guy in their lives and their relationship problems. As I said earlier, I always hung out with adults growing up, so these women also confided in me every dirty detail. I saw videotapes in which they performed in "sexiest legs" contests in the clubs, which my mom always won, of course. The downside: many of them dated married men and also were in seriously abusive relationships. I watched as they tried to put makeup on a black eye, or reduce swelling in a busted lip. I saw a lot of fights and violence between couples. It scared me to death, and I decided I never wanted a relationship like that.

Although my dad never hit me, my mother was quite abusive. She would yell, scream, hit, and kick when I didn't conform to her will. I was afraid of her, but in a different way. With my father, it was more of a fear of disappointing him, but with my mother, it was a fear of getting hit or punished. Everyone knew that my mother didn't play, and her temper was well-known. She was violent like this in her adult relationships as well; very jealous, likely stemming from her fear of abandonment. If a man she was with talked to another woman, or even laughed with even his own family members, she would fly into a rage and punch, kick, throw a chair at him. My dad tells me that he and my mom fought viciously even when she was pregnant with me, so fighting to this day stresses me out. My dad jokingly says, "You had no choice but to beat her up, because if not, she kept coming at you with whatever she can get her hands on." Obviously domestic violence laws were not in affect like they are today. I witnessed her doing this a few times, so I never saw her as an abuse victim, but rather a woman who will punch you in the face first and ask questions later. She was blunt and no one dared to cross her. To this day, I will still try to never disrespect her out of a fear instilled from my childhood.

I was also the babysitter for all of the women while they clubbed. One of my mother's friends was dating the husband of another one. They all knew it...well, everyone but the poor wife. I would actually watch the kids for both of them while they ran off having their affair. But I was more than the babysitter. I would pretend that these were my own children. I would cook for them, do their hair, dress them up, put on performances with them, and create an imaginary family with these children. Many of them were as stressed as I was over the adults in our lives, and they always told me they wanted me to be their mother. I spent time reading to them, talking to them, and teaching them lesson plans. I knew I wanted a large family, so these children became my family. I didn't much relate to kids my own age because I thought they were silly and immature. So, these babysitting jobs were a way for me to feel motherly and important. I looked forward to being with the kids as much as they did me. I became the mother they were lacking, and they became my pseudo-family...minus the husband, whom I simply made up.

Sadly, through all of the relationships I witnessed, I never saw honor and loyalty within a couple—and this was all normal. I started to think such things simply did not exist...but I wanted that for myself. In my imaginations, my husband was strong, loyal, and a leader who adored me and our children. During my childhood, I witnessed a lot of damaging things, and although I was the person everyone told their secrets and heartaches to, I had no one to talk to or vent to myself, or with whom to express my internal longings and desires.

The adults in my life were so busy dealing with drama and relationships that many times I was a sympathetic observer in their lives, and felt extremely lonely and outcast from their real-life adventures. I had nowhere to take my fears, my dreams, and my goals. And so I started to dream and use my imagination, and at age nine, I started to write, and books became my blessed escape.

CHAPTER 2

Hidden Away

I GREW UP LIVING IN TWO WORLDS, essentially, neither of which was particularly wholesome. My parents seemed to love me in their own ways, but the lives they were leading kept them busy—and occupied. They were young when they had me. My mom was trying to establish her career, and my dad was raising a new family, and I was left to my own devices a lot.

I was a gifted child who, thankfully, learned how to read at age two. I don't ever remember learning; I just always knew how. By the time I was in fourth grade, I tested at twelfth grade reading level. I was always enrolled in gifted classes and Montessori schools. In their absences, my parents provided me with lots of learning tools— hundreds of books, hundreds of records, a record player, tape recorder testing kits. These things kept me company and fueled my imagination for many years. Through books, I was comforted and transported to different worlds where young brave kids could overcome odds, be loved, and have two parents who cared for them. Pippi Longstocking was my favorite TV character, a self-reliant and creative young girl who was raising herself and was strong and willful. My favorite movie was *Annie*, about a young orphan seeking the love of a parent.

I had a couple of favorite heroines in books: Helen Keller, who was born blind and deaf in a world that didn't understand her, and who overcame tremendous odds to be someone who mattered; and Anne Frank, who was hidden away in an attic, yet was very creative and positive about her life, and dreamed of a bright future. I read about these characters over and over again, and felt that I could relate to them in some way, and I drew from their strength, courage, and wisdom. One of my books I loved to read was a little orange children's Bible that I got from some traveling Jehovah's Witnesses when I was young. I read those stories repeatedly, and that's how I learned my first lessons about God. Growing up, no one discussed God with me or ever took me to church. But there was something to those stories that made me feel a sense of peace. When the Bible said that you could go to heaven for being good and decent, that's what I wanted. The people in the pictures there seemed happy all the time. I also spent lots of time making up imaginary worlds and wrote my own books and stories. The characters became my friends, and they never left me, unlike the people around me. I read books all day, every day. In my writings I created a husband, children, and an entire imaginary life, and I was determined one day to have that—I just wasn't sure how.

~~~~~~~~

Over the years through my research on the subject of "Purpose," I have discovered a general truth that seems to be similar across the board—that our lives and interests as a young person are tied to our life's purpose. The things that you gravitated toward, the stories you liked to read as a child, the imaginative games you played—all of these things are key in helping to determine what God has for you. My love of books, and teaching other kids, creating games, and seeking knowledge really impacted me later in life. Though I didn't know it at the time, these things that happened in my earlier life laid the foundation for my experiences in creating programs, teaching, and understanding what goes on in the minds of people who are raised under dysfunctional circumstances.

I love strawberries. They are one of my favorite fruits. When I was younger, my favorite character was Strawberry Shortcake, and I had everything in the collection because my grandmother's only grandchild was me, and she therefore spoiled me on my birthdays and Christmases. She also would buy strawberries from the grocery store, wash them, cut them up, and sprinkle sugar on them and then leave them in the fridge overnight. The next day, she would make strawberry shortcakes with whipped cream and ice cream. Yum! It was one of my favorite desserts of hers.

Strawberries start off as these itty bitty tiny seeds that look nothing like the finished product. When you are looking to grow strawberries, you must cultivate the ground and buy the seeds. You don't eat the seeds; they won't taste like strawberries. You place them in the ground, provide water, sunlight, and nourishment for that seed. You then WAIT through any conditions that may arise: winters, birds, and insects. When the seedling starts to sprout, neither do you impatiently yank it out of the ground. Patience is key to getting the finished product. Once you have the strawberry fully grown, you don't just pluck it and set it on your counter for decoration. Why? It will rot, and you will have wasted that time growing those strawberries. No, instead you use it for the purpose intended, which in my case was terrific strawberry shortcake. It was not wasted because I ate it—that was its purpose!

In life we are all born for a purpose, but sometimes we jump ahead of God or resent the growing process. There are things that need to happen before we are ready to fulfill our purpose, and many times these things are actually required so that we will be able to complete our purpose. There were many things I saw, and that were done to me that I didn't understand at the time, but like the strawberry, I realize now that God was preparing me, growing me, and shaping me in service of the purpose that he had for me. He does that with us all, yet we despise the lessons and the struggle. We want life to be easy. Every trial, every horrible situation, and every seeming setback makes us who we are today. And in the end, it is never about US. It's so that we can bless and empower others with our story.

But let patience have her perfect work, that you may be perfect and entire, wanting nothing (James 1:4).

When I was eight years old, I decided to leave my mother and go live with my dad. I was basically a latchkey kid raising myself, and the loneliness and fear at night, along with her violent relationships and worry when she was missing, had finally gotten to me. While she worked and partied, I had to cook for myself and do my own laundry. She kept herself perfectly groomed and expensively dressed, but my hair was matted and my clothing substandard. While she went on vacations and met exciting people, I collected the "Wish You Were Here" postcards she sent me, and stayed constantly alone. I honestly do not remember ever getting a single kiss, or hug from my mother as a child. Even when I had asthma attacks while in school and I was rushed to the hospital, she wasn't there. I once had to go home with a hospital nurse late into the night—a woman I didn't know—because they couldn't find my mother to come and pick me up. Nowadays, Social Services probably would have gotten involved, but those days it wasn't so common to call them. I was tired of raising myself. Although I don't think my mother was a bad person, I just think at the time that she was young, and not ready to be a mother. But what I needed at the time was love, attention, and companionship. Although my dad's home had a different kind of dysfunction, it was always filled with people; my "stepmother" was always there with us kids, and my dad was very affectionate and great fun. I chose what I considered the lesser of two evils.

Living with my father and his girlfriend was the best year of my life. There were dozens of kids in the neighborhood, and I had plenty of freedom, and friends to play with daily. My dad's other two kids provided me with a little sister and brother, which I loved, and I really started to feel like a normal kid. The only drawback was that my dad's wild ways caused him to miss taking me to school a lot. He would wake up, come into my room, and just ask me if I felt like going to school that day. Hey, I'm a kid...most times, I was like, well, *no*! I missed a majority of the fourth grade. My father thought it was no big deal—he taught me a lot at home. But, my mother was livid when she saw my first D on a report card. She soon came up with a plan of her own: to get me away from my father forever.

Here's what happened: When I was nine, my mom and her sister came to pick me up from Dad's house saying they were taking me school clothes shopping. They really went all out! They got me all kinds of stuff: matching shoes, hair accessories, socks, things I never had (I was always a bit of a ragamuffin). So I was really happy about this trip. Then at one point they gave me a choice: *we can stop and take you home right now, or you can stay and go shopping with us longer.* Excited about getting new clothes, I chose to stay.

Little did I know that I wouldn't see my dad again for six years, and that I would be taken to live with my aunt in a room inside a home she lived in with a sixty-year-old man.

This man, Jim*, and my aunt did not seem to like each other much, and the tension would carry over into their communication with each other. Jim owned an auto mechanic shop, and would often come home from work intoxicated; the two of them would curse each other out at least once or twice a week. I stayed there for two years, not understanding why on earth I was there. I was disappointed and miserable. It was the opposite of Dad's house. My aunt was often stressed, and seemed to be unhappy in her situation. She had a short fuse and yelled at me a lot, grabbed me, hit me. It started to make me feel stressed as well. Although she was my mother's only sibling, it seemed she hated BOTH of my parents, and I was forced to listen to her gossip with friends for hours on end about my mother and her abusive boyfriend of the moment. It would anger me, because I still looked up to both of them and as a child could not defend them verbally. She showed me police reports that my mother had filed and she angrily said, "You think your parents are so perfect, but they are NOTHING." This remains burned in my memory as a source of great pain. However, when my mother came around, my aunt seemed nice, and sisterly.

My aunt was a chain smoker, too, and I was an asthmatic: bad combination. I made multiple trips to the hospital during the two years I lived there. And there were mice everywhere, which I was deathly afraid of. Although the main part of the house was usually clean, the room that my aunt and I shared was filled with clothes and items often piled high to the point where we could barely move around. Back then I didn't know why the room was so packed, but today, thanks to television shows, I now know that she was a hoarder. This added another element to my stress, because I didn't know where the mice would pop out at any time. As a survival measure, many nights I slept in the living room on the couch to avoid my bed, where the high pile of clothes next to it allowed mice to climb up in bed with me—once I even woke up when one ran across my face. As a child, I was petrified in a way that still haunts me today in nightmares. Don't get me wrong, I love my aunt dearly, and I don't think she was a bad person, but just extremely unhappy and lonely, and had an emotional impairment that caused her to feel unloved, and want to hold onto and control items, and the memories that came with them. I felt that even as a young girl. Although extremely beautiful, she had gained a lot of weight in her early twenties, and this may have affected her self-esteem. I think in some ways she felt a competition with my mother when they were younger, and somehow felt my mother was the "favored" child. At one point I also discovered that my aunt had had a short-lived physical relationship with my father (before my mother came along) and perhaps that contributed to some of the animosity that I felt from her towards the two of them.

Although I appreciated the fact that my aunt cared for me for several years, I didn't want to be there, and I just really wanted to go back to live with my dad. At one point, I decided that I would even take mom's house. But they didn't let me leave, although I begged my mother repeatedly. My mother still denies it, but I think she was actually hiding me from my dad. My dad tells me now that I was basically *kidnapped* and he had no idea where I was. To be fair, both my mother and aunt deny this, and both say that he knew where I was; he just didn't visit me (which, given our history of closeness, was pretty hard for me to believe). She said she sent me to live with my aunt for my protection—she wanted me away from drug dealers and criminals, and my grades were slipping. Now that I am a parent I can see it from her point of view, and am sure that she felt strongly and had her reasons. But at the time, I didn't understand why she didn't take me to live with her. She says she was involved in an abusive relationship (as usual) and didn't want me to see it. So instead, I lived for two years with my aunt and Jim.

In addition to the piles of clothes and items that packed the walls and floors in the small room we shared, my aunt owned a huge Afghan hound dog that stayed in the room with us, too…and he carried fleas. So you can picture the chaos and filth: fleas, mice, and clothes everywhere. She seemed to want to hold onto everything. Perhaps it was that she felt that she had no control…maybe she felt connected to her possessions. I'm not sure what goes on in the mind of those who hoard, but every few months my mother would come over and take a week or two to help her clean our room again. My aunt wasn't a bad guardian; she did her best to do things for me, she just had her own problems, and—living conditions notwithstanding—she seemed to care about me very much. She had no children of her own, and I think in a way she felt I was the child she couldn't have. We went on several trips together, which I never did with my own mother, and she spoiled me with material things, even though on her limited income she could clearly not afford it. She gave me my first experience leaving California when she took me to Canada to visit our distant relatives. She loaded me down with Cabbage Patch Kids paraphernalia, lots of clothes and games, and she did my hair very nicely, and dressed me to a tee. Like never in life, I was looking great; I matched like nobody's business!

While I appeared neat and clean on the outside, on the inside I was miserable, living in one room in a house with what in my young mind was a chain smoking, angry woman. Although, again, to be fair, there were good moments as well; she bought me many nice things, kept me nicely dressed, and was truly involved with my education. She spent a lot of time with me, and made sure that I ate properly, and was healthy. She was very creative, and made sure my schoolwork was done well, and I got straight A's the two years that I stayed with her. She once helped me put together a beautiful family tree that spanned five generations back to Ireland. She often allowed my friends to visit, bought us matching pajamas and treated them well, often letting us have slumber parties, and even fun camping trips that she prepared for with every supply known to man. She created "Good" and "Bad" Behavior Tickets for me and Jim's granddaughters, who were frequent visitors to the home, and we were rewarded or punished based on what we did around the house. She could write calligraphy beautifully, and read every V.C. Andrews, Stephen King and other romance novels by the dozen, which she shared with me, starting my love of novels and psychological thrillers.

On the flip side, she had an extremely dominant personality, yelled at me often, disrespected my parents viciously, which hurt my feelings, and fought at least once a week with the Jim, who owned the house, which made life there at times feel unbearable to a sensitive child such as myself. Jim was a soft spoken and kind man during the day, and I liked him. He showed me how to plant flowers, and took me fishing. However, at night when he came home from work intoxicated, he seemed to be ready to fight. I hated fighting and violence. I still don't know why my aunt lived in his house; I was once told they were a couple, which surprised me, because in two years, I never saw them talk nicely to each other or even share a room more than a handful of times. She shared a room with me, and he had his own room. (There was a third bedroom, but she used it to store the items that wouldn't fit in our room.) I never saw them hug or kiss each other even once.

Jim was about twenty-five years older than my aunt. He was very nice and sweet to me, but when he drank, he drank a lot, and his personality became angry, and he would stand in the doorway to our room nightly, begging my aunt to come to his room and "lay with him." It made me uncomfortable because during these times, he didn't seem to notice that I was there. My aunt would scream at him to leave her alone, and he often felt so angry at her rejections that they would launch into a full scale verbal battle. The atmosphere became so volatile at times, that he once pulled a gun during a fight with my aunt. I was forced to call the police during a fist fight or two. I was always shaking and terrified when the fights started. The only thing that got me through this time in my life was the fact that, as I mentioned, the Jim had two young granddaughters my age, who came over and played with me often. I never told them what was going on, and we became best friends. Jim and my aunt never fought when they came over, so I tried to keep the girls over often. They girls were mouthy, and headstrong and didn't get along as much with my aunt, but she couldn't stop them from being there since they were his grandkids. They knew this, and made sure that they came over as much as possible. I loved going over their house too. Their parents had five kids total and it was a loud and rambunctious bunch, and I loved the chaotic family atmosphere, and wanted that for myself someday. My aunt enrolled me in a local school with these girls, so I didn't feel so alone and out of place. It was my fifth grade year when I moved into this situation, and I was almost ten.

Sometimes, even in the midst of what seems like a horrible situation and a mistake, God can make sure that you come to know him. (In fact, these are often the times when we look to him because we have no one else.) Looking back, I now see an obvious plan in all of this. I didn't know it at the time, but shortly after I left my dad's house, he found out that his abusive father who raised him was really only his stepfather. This sent him spiraling out of control in anger and self-destruction. He went from selling drugs, to using them. Perhaps God took me out of that situation because who-knows-what could have happened to me while my dad was high.

In the midst of all the changes in my life I was adjusting to, I started a new school with Jim's granddaughters, located in the middle of south central Los Angeles. At my new school I was assigned a teacher who made such an impact on my life that I would never be the same. Miss Cherry White was a pretty, fair skinned African American woman and an extremely devout Christian, even during a time when you were not allowed to talk about Christ in the schools. Miss White didn't seem to care about those rules. She talked about the Lord freely, and even had all of our parents sign waivers to allow corporal punishment (which wasn't even used in California). She never had to *use* the paddle, but just the threat kept us on our toes. Instead Miss White would get on her knees and pray loudly for us when we were unruly, which caused everyone to feel bad and stop acting up in class. Miss White taught us Christian songs in English and Spanish, and she invited any of us to stay in at lunch time to learn the Bible if we wanted to. Usually I and two or three others would stay. I had a hunger to know who God was. I didn't have religious guidance. Mom claimed to be an atheist and Dad never really claimed anything. So I was left to my own devices. Besides my little children's Bible, I was literally a blank slate when it came to religion.

Miss White took me to church and a fire was lit under me. I still can't explain why I just KNEW in my heart that Christianity was the right way. It didn't make much sense to me, since I'd never had any formal religious teaching whatsoever. I was exposed to many forms of religion. My aunt was Buddhist, so I was taken to Buddhist meetings with her, but I would cover my ears and face at the back of the room while they chanted. In my mind, even at a young age, I felt that these people were worshipping a *false god* and I wanted no part of it. I don't even know how I knew what a false god was. Jehovah's Witnesses frequently visited the house, and my aunt invited them in, so we talked to them as well. I felt they were slightly off with their theories of Jesus and the Trinity, but I didn't know *why* I felt these things.

If you have no idea who God is, I think it's easier to find out, because you have no preconceived 'religious' notions, and He sends people in your life to help you discover Him. Miss White just seemed to be a perfect example of love, patience, and tolerance. She smiled and encouraged, and talked about Jesus all the time. It just felt right. When I went to church with Miss White, I felt at home for some reason. When I found out my father went to jail that year, I was devastated. But comfort came through the songs of Miss White, her loving words, and the compassion she showed. After Miss White left, my aunt saw that I missed church and she did something that really made an impact: she started taking me to a teen Christian youth church called Maranatha, in Los Angeles. She never stayed or went in; every Friday she dropped me off out front, and picked me up after the teen "Friday Night Live" service was over. I had so much fun in that group that even after I left my aunt's house and moved back on my mother, amazingly, she would still come and get me each Friday and take me to L.A. for a few months afterward. It's there that I learned a lot about God and got a lot of my questions answered. The hip music and rap contests kept my attention, and made it fun as well.

The Bible says that sometimes you can entertain strangers as angels unaware. Out of everyone I've met, if I had to pick someone, I would think that Miss Cherry White may have been an angel. I can't prove it and it may sound silly, but she seemed to have simply disappeared after she taught my fifth grade class. I can't find her anywhere, and word was that she stopped teaching after that year to become a traveling missionary. I tried to Google her and it reported that she was living in a nearby city, on a street named *Prosperity Lane*. But when I tried the phone number, it was disconnected. None of the former students from our class ever heard from her again after that year. You never know who you affect, and the seed she planted in me still remains with me to this day. God later sent others into my life to water it.

One day around that time, I remember so clearly that I was standing in the middle of the schoolyard by myself and I started to plan my future. I started talking to God and I told him exactly what I wanted. Miss White had talked about the power of prayer, so I put it to the test: I asked God for a husband and five kids. I stated the exact order of the genders I wanted, and said, *"God, if you give me these kids I will raise them to know You."* Little did I know, years later, I would get exactly what I prayed for, and more.

~~~~~~

Now, almost ten years later, as I waited for my scheduled abortion appointment, these memories came flooding back and made me feel extremely uneasy, and guilty. Was I taking the life of a child who was prayed for long ago? Or was I correcting a mistake that, later on when I was married and stable, I could make right?

CHAPTER 3

Options

FAST-FORWARD TO THE PRESENT: Here I am, pregnant with baby number two. *How did I get in this position again?* I wondered.

~~~~~~~

For a while, before this unexpected pregnancy, my future was beginning to look up. Several months earlier I had taken my infant son and gone from California, (where I had been living with my dad again after his release from prison) moving to Georgia to live with my mother. My boyfriend was playing college basketball and was living in a dorm, and things were too hectic with my dad. He had been to prison twice, and had changed from "fun/party dad" to "angry bitter sober man with bills and problems." We were both suprised to find that we no longer got along once he got released: I had grown into a strong-willed fifteen-year-old, and was no longer the little nine-year-old girl who blindly idolized him. I had gone back to live with him as soon as he got out of prison, when I was fifteen years old, but sadly, things were never the same. He had me and his son living with him, and he yelled and screamed all the time. He could yell for two hours over a water spot in the floor, or a stain on the coffee table. I'm not sure what changed for him internally during his time in jail, but it hurt me to have him yell and curse me, and I cried often, and mentally retreated into a shell, eventually hardening my heart against him. I honestly felt like I lost my dad in the six years that we were apart, and when he was in prison.

It was 1991, I was seventeen years old and my mother was excited to have me and my three-month-old son there—my first born, Gerald II—with her in Georgia. She had pulled strings to have me enrolled in Spellman University, a prestigious African American all-women's college in Atlanta, and I was planning to start in the spring of 1992. My mother and I arranged for childcare for my son, and things were seemingly on the right track for me. I felt like even though I was a teen mom, I was on track to being a success. My only problem was that I was still in love with, and separated from, my son's father Gerald, who still lived on the other side of the U.S., back in California.

Despite our issues, being young parents, and not fully understanding the responsibilities, Gerald had been a fairly good dad to our son. He seemed to really love him, calling and checking on him constantly when we were apart, and he had always been affectionate, hugging and kissing him generously. He had never known or met his own dad growing up, so he wanted to be different with his own son. I wanted him to stay involved in his son's life and always sent him videos of the baby eating, bathing, and crawling for the first time. I hated and felt guilty about the fact that he was missing out. Our plans were to get an education and then hopefully be together down the line. We had discussed marriage, but it wasn't on Gerald's list of immediate goals. He didn't seem ready to have that discussion, ever; we argued about it quite often. He said I was rushing things, but I felt like a baby should have two stable parents in a marriage. However, while I was in Georgia, he sent me nice letters and called constantly, telling me that he loved and missed us. I saved the letters, and cherished every word.

When a tree is planted, its roots grow in the direction of whatever is going to give it nourishment, whether healthy or toxic. In our own lives, we often seek love and acceptance from the very people who may hurt and/or abuse us. Often, I felt as if making Gerald love me and see my value was an accomplishment. Gerald was handsome and charismatic, and what I always called "the life of the party." He had a group of single friends and was still out with them "sowing his wild oats," drinking, partying, listening to rap music, and being a sought after college ballplayer who became fifth in the nation for scoring. He was getting lots of attention from coaches and scouts, who felt he didn't need to be committed to anything but basketball. He was confident, sometimes to the point of arrogance, and often we would argue about me feeling neglected, and the fact that he wouldn't send money, or items for the baby. Looking back, although we felt like adults, at seventeen and twenty years old, I am not sure that neither of us were truly ready for the commitment and responsibilities we were facing as young parents trying to reach our goals. But parenting an active baby was a stressful twenty-four hour a day job for me, and I needed his support. Since my parents often were not available, I needed someone to be there for me who could fill that void—and I wanted to make the family unit work, however toxic the relationship often was.

In November, I told my mother that before I started college, I wanted to take the baby to visit Gerald. We had been away from him for four months by this time, and a baby goes through a huge change from three to seven months. I didn't want little Gerald to not know who his dad was. I missed Gerald as well, and he had been asking me when we would be visiting, saying he wanted to see his son.

We took a plane to see him. Gerald was excited to seeing me and the baby again, and we had a wonderful reunion. I didn't know that I would actually end up pregnant before the visit ended. The trip was supposed to be about three weeks, but I suspected I was pregnant within two. My body worked like clockwork, and I knew that when nausea replaced a period, then there was a red flag.

I was horrified, and so disappointed! Now, here I was, stuck in California, unable to go back to Georgia, because I couldn't bring myself to tell my mother I had gotten pregnant again. Yes, we used condoms, which I had always been told were pretty much a hundred percent guaranteed. I didn't learn that they were unreliable *until they failed me*. What a lesson to learn! I cried for days. As hard as it was, I called my mother and just lied to her. I told her I was staying because Gerald wanted to be with his son, and although she was devastated, she respected my decision. We had just really started to mend our relationship and get closer, mostly due to the fact that she was such an attentive and amazing grandmother to my baby. There was nothing she wouldn't buy or do for him, and it was such a switch from my own childhood, that it made me feel really good about the fact that she was becoming more of a family person. She wrote me a long letter about how much she loved me and hated to see me leave, and just wanted the best for me and my son, which made me cry. I still have that letter to this day. So when I found myself pregnant, and confirmed it with a home pregnancy test, I thought that maybe if I got an abortion then I could just go back to Georgia, and go back to school.

Gerald said he would support any decision I made regarding an abortion. He was my first real love—I started dating him when I was only fifteen years old. When I met him in tenth grade, I already had a boyfriend, and at the time Gerald was not really my type. Although he was eighteen, tall, dark, handsome, extremely popular, and a basketball player, I felt he was cocky—too flirty and outgoing, aggressive, had a short attention span, was not too smart, and shockingly rude. He once walked up to me and licked my cheek. I was horrified! He was a ladies' man as well, and in my mind, he was arrogant, and conceited. Several girls were fighting over him at school, and his last girlfriend before me was twenty-seven years old! I was much more reserved, rather studious and introverted, and liked long haired, light skinned boys who were intellects, yet gang members, and made me laugh. I also felt I didn't measure up to the girls Gerald had been with who were voluptuous, and sexually experienced. Neither did I want drama at school.

When we first met, Gerald and I disliked each other, and the only reason we started talking was that his closest friend Julian and my close friend Sheila started dating, and fell in love with each other. So we were basically forced to talk to each other daily as a foursome. They encouraged us to date each other, which we initially resisted, but once we got together often enough, we became friends, and once school ended, things quickly progressed from there. He was rather charming, I had to admit. His mother worked two jobs, and at his home I watched him at home cooking, cleaning, and taking care of, discipline, and lovingly teach his younger siblings (one of whom was an infant) while his mother worked two jobs, and I thought he would make a great dad. Soon, we were inseparable; I fell hard, dumped my boyfriend, and never looked back.

Another one of the things that attracted me to Gerald was the fact that he seemed different. At the time I lived in Compton, California, which is home of the 'gangster-rap' movement, and it was in full swing at this time. Many guys in our area were "thugs," dressed in sweat suits, sagging jeans, and long white tees, or silk shirts and corduroys. Gerald, however, would come to school like he was dressed for church, in dress pants, turtlenecks, and dressy sandals. He appeared to take pride in his appearance, which I found attractive. He didn't pretend to be tough, but most of the gangsters would not harass him because he was a fighter, born and raised in the projects of Memphis, and was very quick to show other guys that he was not to be messed with. On several occasions he had a gun pulled on him and still managed to intimidate the shooter, once even knocking him unconscious. Julian was a golden gloves boxer, and even though teens, they both quickly earned respect. The local thugs left them alone, and they didn't have any gang affiliations. Gerald reminded me of my father, in the respect that he was fearless and strong. But unlike my dad, he never smoked, or drank, which I admired.

Once he expressed his physical interest in me, I also was under intense pressure to be attractive to him in *every way*. Girls were coming at him left and right. I had decided a few years earlier that I wanted to wait until marriage to have sex. With the few months of church I had experienced living with my aunt, I had learned that abstinence until marriage was God's will. Though at this point I still wasn't saved, or part of a church, I still respected the biblical views and also wanted to be different from my friends, and I thought virginity sounded like a great idea.

Once Gerald and I became a couple, we spent a lot of time alone together. Like any eighteen year old male, he moved really quickly in trying to take our relationship to the next level. Naturally so, since he had already been intimate in that way since he was fourteen years old. However, I wasn't ready, so it took many nights of his begging, pleading, and finally, declarations of "love", to convince me that he was "the one." It took over a year of convincing, in fact, (which is an eternity to teenagers) but I eventually, hesitantly, gave him my virginity.

The very first time was scary, painful, and not at all what I expected, but it was enough to change my life; I got pregnant that night. Over those first few pregnant months the pressure seemed to be getting to him. I was surprised that while I was going through the shock and horror of my condition, his attitude quickly changed from loving boyfriend, to nonchalant guy who I just happened to have had sex with. Then he disappeared for five months.

It was the loneliest time of my life. I endured the pregnancy alone, hiding it from my friends and family, until I was seven months pregnant, when finally Gerald decided he wanted to be involved. During the separation, however, he was discovered to be unfaithful. My heart was crushed, my trust shattered, and I didn't feel I could rely on him to really be there for me in the long run. In my mind, I felt he was no better than all those guys my dad and his friends had warned me about…and I beat myself up internally: *How didn't I see it coming?* I was ashamed and angry beyond words. I regretted giving him my virginity and didn't speak to him for several weeks. But I remembered that there was also a child now involved, and I didn't want to be a single teen mother—so I forgave and stayed with him but never really felt I could count on anyone—especially him. This betrayal, and my subsequent lack of trust affected our relationship for many years afterward.

~~~~~~~~~~~

Since my first pregnancy with him had been so traumatic and the relationship felt so unstable, when I found myself pregnant again (when my son was only seven months old), my mind was made up—

I was having this abortion. There was no way I felt that I could bring another child into an already unstable situation.

As part of my abortion requirement, I had to obtain a pregnancy test. Of course, I had no money. I didn't work at the time. I was out of school and was supposed to go to college. In my search for a place to do a pregnancy test, I chose a crisis pregnancy clinic. This seemed to fit with my situation: a crisis. The Yellow Pages ad said that they gave free pregnancy tests. That was very much within my budget. I set an appointment for a test. The people were really sweet and sounded caring. Much more so than the abortion clinic worker, who seemed irritated and rushed me off the phone.

When I went to take the test, Gerald came with me. Everyone smiled and welcomed me. I noticed the walls were decorated with pictures of happy pregnant women, and laughing babies. I started to feel somewhat guilty but I knew my plans were set. We met with a person who said she was a mentor and that she would be giving me the test. Once the three of us were in the private room, I told her I needed the test because I was considering getting an abortion. She asked me why I felt the need to do that, and I explained it was my only option. I had no money, my boyfriend was in college, I was only eighteen, I already had a one-year-old, and I would be unable to tell my mother or to go to college if I had a baby. All seemed to be valid reasons to me, and I was sure the lady would understand that this wasn't just a rash decision on my part. The lady, however, proceeded to tell me that God loved me and my baby and that there were options, and that they would be able to help me if I would allow them to.

I felt irritated that she didn't seem to agree with me that my situation was hopeless, and I reminded her I needed my test taken, and added that I was in a hurry. I peed in the supplied cup and while I waited for the results, they asked if they could play a short film for me, and Gerald and I agreed.

When they left, I felt both annoyed and offended. Although they were sweet and friendly and in no way said anything negative about my choice, in my mind they were making me feel *bad* about my decision. The film showed different abortion procedures, and talked about how it was taking the *life* of a person. I already knew all that—I just honestly didn't care enough to let it change my mind. As far as I was concerned, this child would take MY life too. So we were even.

Gerald and I even joked during the abortion film and commented that they couldn't change our minds. In the film they kept talking about helping us, but we knew they weren't going to give us diapers, feed our kids, provide a roof over our heads, or give us money! How could they really help us? That's the kind of help we needed. We didn't say those things out loud to them, but we surely didn't take them seriously either. I just wanted my test so I could leave and go do what I had to do.

I do remember, though, that when they talked to me about God, and the sweetness and love she expressed, it piqued my interest. I wasn't raised to even know who God was, but in the back of my mind I always had a desire to get to know Him, and for some reason I was always drawn to people who displayed a love of God. It stirred memories of my little Gold Jehovah's Witness children's Bible…and Miss White's loving prayers stirred deep within me.

CHAPTER 4

Fork in the Road

THE DAY BEFORE my scheduled abortion appointment, everything was set. Gerald had obtained his sister's Medicaid card, I had all of my instructions written down, and he even came over to spend the night with me so we could make SURE we weren't late for the appointment. I was so nervous but still had very little doubt that this was something I really wanted to do. I was ill all the time with morning sickness, and felt that this baby already made me tired and resentful. My son was a very active little boy with no seeming limit to his energy level. He was always jumping around, hyper, and into everything. I would often take him to friends' houses and just fall dead asleep with him running wild, tearing up their things. I felt so exhausted all the time and just wanted to be myself again. On top of that, another girl came forward with stories of my boyfriend being unfaithful, and Gerald and I were fighting like cats and dogs. I knew too that time was passing quickly, and soon I would feel the baby kicking, and it would be hard for me to have an abortion once I knew that the baby was actually "real"—at this point, I could be in denial and see it as a huge blob of blood. Gerald seemed cool with whatever decision I made, as his life hadn't changed much anyway with the arrival of my son. I still took sole care of my son, and Gerald still got to go to college and pursue his dreams and live his life.

Finally, the day for the abortion arrived. Early in the morning on the day of the scheduled procedure, Gerald's pager went off. It was about 7 a.m., almost time for him to get up and take me to the clinic. He said the call was his aunt from Victorville, which was unusual because she never called him that early. When he called her back, she told him that she needed him to come over and help her move some furniture—at 7 a.m. I told him he needed to let her know we had PLANS and that he could help her afterward, at the latest 10. Yet he never liked telling his family no about anything, so he told me he HAD to go help her, and to reschedule my appointment. I was extremely angry. I felt like he let me down...again.

"In his heart a man plans his course, but the LORD determines his steps"
(Proverbs 16:9).

Little did I know that during this time, although I had a plan in my mind of how I wanted things to play out, it seems God had other plans. As much as it sometimes frustrates us when things don't go the way we planned, sometimes God may be closing a door, and giving us the opportunity to make a different decision. God will often make it difficult for us to choose a wrong path. Obstacles may hit us left and right out of nowhere, and we can't understand WHY, and we resent the obstacles. We see these obstacles as a negative thing, instead of a supernatural act of a loving Father who does not want to see us wander down a dangerous path. Many people recite the phrase "God won't give us more than we can handle," but that's nowhere in the Bible. Actually, what the Bible says is that *"No temptation has overtaken you except what is common to mankind. And God is faithful; he will not let you be **tempted beyond** what you can bear. But when you are tempted, **he will also provide a way out** so that you can endure it."* Here, it seems that even in the midst of my pressing forward on *my plans*, God was still working to provide a way out.

I have no idea why God chose to work in my life that day. I wasn't anyone special, and I wasn't living for Him. But perhaps we are *all* *s*pecial to Him. The Bible says He will leave the ninety-nine sheep to go after the one lost sheep, and I was definitely lost, and on the path to following those before me. As tender as my heart was, God knew that guilt would eat me up for years by going through with this abortion, causing me to possibly turn to drugs and /or alcohol to soothe the pain. I have no idea why He came to the rescue of the lost girl who really just needed her daddy. But He did, and He lined things up to make sure my plans were derailed—not taking away my free will but giving me an OUT so that I had another chance to make a different choice—a better choice.

Sometimes the way out is just the ability to leave the room. Sometimes it's the voice or advice of a friend. Sometimes, it's a timely call at seven in the morning from an aunt needing assistance moving. Look for God sending you your Way Out, and don't despise it. He loves you and wants to protect you. Even I, who didn't have God in my life, was still getting my way out. The question was—would I take it?

I angrily called the abortion clinic, intent on rescheduling my appointment. Just as I suspected, the lady on the line sounded annoyed and even insulted that I wasn't showing up. I explained my situation.

"Well, you don't have much time. If you get too much further, the price goes up. This is already a harder procedure because you are farther along, into your second trimester."

"Yes, sorry. My boyfriend had an emergency. Can we please just reschedule?"

Sigh.

"Yeah, just come Thursday at the same time."

"Thank you so much."

Click.

I felt embarrassed. Now this lady can see what a young, irresponsible girl I am that I can't even keep a simple appointment. I silently cursed myself—and Gerald.

Why wouldn't anything just be easy? I thought.

A few days later, I just happened to be lying around thinking about the video I had watched about the abortion. This lady said it would be a harder procedure. Did that mean that the baby would feel pain? Would it cry and scream? Would it scar me where I couldn't have kids in the future? Would I be sad for years afterward, like several women I knew who even had nightmares about their dead babies, and severe guilt? I again remembered the nice, non-judgmental attitudes of the people who worked at the crisis pregnancy center; they didn't judge me or even seem annoyed.

As a matter of fact, they had given me a brochure showing me the exact stage of development my baby was in. I kept looking at it. At four months, the baby was almost seven inches long, with hands, feet, a beating heart. It can smile, frown, and even cry and suck its thumb.

An ultrasound can sometimes determine at this stage if it was a boy or girl. I never even got to the point of thinking it could be one or the other. But how could I ever tell my parents? And at this point, I moved out of my dad's house and was staying at a girlfriend's of my dad's, watching her newborn twin babies, my new little sisters. I had watched this woman grieve because my dad would not leave his new, rich, stable girlfriend to be with her and her babies, and she was raising them alone; I didn't want to end up like that. I offered to help while she went to work in exchange for a place to stay. But my son and I slept in her room on the hard floor, and she never bought me food. I was basically homeless and taking care of her twins, and my son. Being pregnant, hungry, and uncomfortable was really wearing on me.

I went back through the Yellow Pages and found the Crisis Center, listed under "Abortion Alternatives." I remembered they had said that if I kept my baby, they would help me in any way they could. I thought to myself, well, my appointment isn't until tomorrow, so it can't hurt to SEE what they can do for me, right? That's all I was going to do, I reasoned,—just see my options.

In order to make a fully informed decision, you should know ALL of your options. That is key in good decision-making. The lady at the abortion clinic, I noticed, never once offered me an *option* or an *alternative*. She didn't even ask me WHY I wanted an abortion. She didn't seem concerned about my mental well-being, nor about giving me any information about the developing baby other than calling it a "pregnancy" in an "advanced state." On the other hand, the people from the crisis pregnancy clinic seemed caring and genuine, as if they not only cared about the baby but also about my well-being. They let me know in no uncertain terms that whatever decision I made, they

wanted to help me through it, and even if I chose an abortion, I could get post-abortion counseling to deal with any grief that may arise.
I dialed the number.

"Heartbeat Ministries…How may I help you?" said the pleasant voice on the other end.

Tears sprang to my eyes immediately.

"My name is Myckelle Riggins, and I came in there last week for a pregnancy test. I don't know who I spoke to, but the lady said that she would be able to help me."

"Yes, what do you need?"

"Well, I don't have a place to live, and I have an eleven-month-old son. I have an appointment for an abortion tomorrow as well.
So the question is….what *can* you do for me?"

Little did I know then that this question—these six little words—would change the entire course of my life and send me hurtling down the path to my destiny.

PART 2

A NEW LIFE

Then took the other, as just as fair,
And having perhaps the better claim
Because it was grassy and wanted wear,
Though as for that the passing there
Had worn them really about the same...

CHAPTER 5

The Hansons

EVERY CHOICE YOU MAKE will either take you closer to your destiny and purpose or farther away from it. Even the small choices have consequences or benefits. Most of the time when we are young, our main interest is to have fun and enjoy life. We figure that we will worry about grown up matters when we grow up. We don't realize that once we start making grownup decisions, we become grown in our own way and sometimes must face grown-up consequences.

Life was no longer easy for me. I was a mother at seventeen years old as the result of ONE TIME choosing to have sex. I now had the responsibility of another human life to grow, raise, and guide, but I still needed to be taken care of myself, too, because I wasn't fully independent. But, unbeknownst to me, God met my needs in His own perfect way. We've all heard the phrase, "God helps those who help themselves," but this phrase is nowhere in the Bible either. What is does say, however, is *Trust in the Lord with all your heart, and lean not on your own understanding; with all your ways acknowledge him and he shall direct your path* (Proverbs 3:5-6).

When we are born into the world, we are totally dependent on our parents. We need them for everything and can't survive without them. As we grow older, we go from dependence to independence. We learn to crawl, walk, run, feed ourselves, then get dressed, tie shoes, and so on. This is how it's designed in the world's system. God's system is the opposite; he desires to take us from *independence* in the world to dependence on Him! He wants us to trust in, lean on, look to and, like the babe, seek all support and nourishment from Him. It's like growing in reverse. That's how you please God—by becoming as an innocent child. Thus, the meaning of the verse that says *"Unless you become like this child, you can't enter the Kingdom"*(Matthew 18:3). God wants us to look to HIM to take total care of us!

Within a week of my phone call, the people from the clinic had located a home for me to live in. They came to my house and picked me up. I went to meet the couple, Karen and David Hanson, and their young children, and we did an interview to determine if it would be a good match.

Upon first meeting, there didn't seem to be anything really spectacular about them. Karen was small and thin, in her mid-thirties, with short, bobbed, mousy brown hair, a ready laugh, sparkling brown eyes, and pretty face. She looked like your typical "PTA mom." David was average height, average weight, mid to late thirties, light brown hair, bearded, and very soft-spoken, with bright blue eyes. He reminded me of the pictures of Jesus in the Bible but with short, cropped hair. He had very kind, piercing eyes and a ready smile. During our interview, I learned that they had been married eleven years. They were apparently childless for seven and then excitedly became parents after much prayer and trying. The two children were girls: Corrine, aged three and Micah age one-and-a-half, both blonde haired little beauties who were a great mix of both parents.

They were—to my surprise, of course—a *white* couple. I had never really lived with white people. I wasn't opposed to it because my maternal grandmother, who I loved dearly (and who died when I was younger), was white, so I knew and corresponded often with some of her family members who still lived in Canada, and was taught how to speak properly as well as be on my best behavior. So that wasn't the issue. The issue was that these people had *gasp* RULES, and at this point I felt that at eighteen years old, with one baby and another on the way, I was "grown up." They along with the representative from the pregnancy center introduced themselves and proceeded to tell me that as part of the agreement, I couldn't watch TV or listen to secular music in their home, or discuss religion or sex with their kids. They also said I couldn't stay out past 10 p.m. and couldn't spend the night at my boyfriend's house. These people also had another requirement: I must go everywhere with them, and attend church with them two to three days per week!

I was flabbergasted. Why would anyone go to church *three days a week*, I wondered? Wasn't Sunday good enough? Was this some sort of cult or brainwashing group? Would they eventually force me to dress in robes, shave my head, and sell flowers at the airport?

Three days in church seemed rather intense. Were these the "Jesus Freaks" my dad had warned my about? My boyfriend, an avid rap fan and pretty prejudiced, just laughed at me. We were hesitant but had no other choices. He lived with family and was in school. There was nowhere else for me to go.

The home was huge, white, traditional, and sat on lots of land. David built the home himself, and it started off as a one-room apartment that was tiny, and he just expanded around it. Now it looked massive and old fashioned, like stepping back into time. Wood floors covered the entire home, and everything was solidly built in two full levels. A huge wooden staircase led to four bedrooms upstairs, including a room for me and my son with two twin-sized cherry wood poster beds and a cherry desk in-between, as well as a bathroom for my personal use. It was nice, and everything seemed antique-like, white and clean. Until I got my financial situation together, they agreed to provide my transportation and meals, as well as any help I needed in getting government assistance, and I would also join them on any trips and outings they took as a family. In essence, I would literally be like another child of theirs.

I hadn't known that there were really programs out there to help women get on their feet. In the beginning, my question had really been more like a dare. A rhetorical question: *What can you do for me?* But it was an eye opening experience. In my mind, I always saw pro-life groups as full of "bull" and wanting control over the life of a woman, standing outside picketing abortion clinics and bombing them as well—a group of weepy, wide-eyed, frizzy-haired radicals who wanted to take away my personal choices. Granted, I never thought abortion was right, but I felt like it was the woman's personal choice and no one else's business. Just like I had joked during the film at the clinic, I rationalized that no one else was going to help her raise that baby, clothe that baby, feed that baby, etc.

I would soon found out how wrong I was. It was explained to me that not only would I be taken in and given a place to live at no cost to me, but I would also receive help with baby items, money to help care for my son, and a home with three meals a day—with nothing asked of me in return except to obey the rules, of course.

So after meeting with the couple, I decided that first I wanted to think about things and decide what I wanted to do. I knew this was a decision of a lifetime—I felt conflicted with so many mixed emotions, but I could feel the significance of this moment. On one hand, I could decline the help that the clinic offered, go through with my scheduled abortion, and continue in my life as I had planned, which possibly included college and a more secure future. On the other hand, I could decide to move in with this unknown family, which would mean that I was choosing to keep my unborn baby, which meant that I would be leaving behind my previous life and looking into an unknown future. I knew that I was facing a crossroads, and I had to quickly choose which way to go. Time was of the essence, and this wasn't an easy decision. I really agonized over it. I only had my boyfriend to discuss it with, and he consistently said that he would support me regardless of my choice. It seemed that the weight of this decision rested squarely on my young shoulders.

Then I thought about all of the women in my family who were single mothers, and those who had had abortions, not really desiring to go down those paths. With the brief amount of Christianity I had encountered, I knew that abortion was fundamentally wrong, and I felt that once I made that decision, I could never take it back. Could I really take the life of a child in order to make my own life more convenient? It was a huge burden for an eighteen-year-old girl to carry.

Finally, I thought that this could possibly be the chance for a different life for me and my son, and I still had that hunger to know God even more than I already did. Did I think that God, or even Miss White would approve of my decisions? There was an internal battle as my heart and my mind argued. Little did I realize that this battle went far beyond even myself in the physical realm. As I sat around thinking of my options I touched my belly, and as I sat very still I felt inside the tiniest fluttering that could easily be mistaken for gas. At fourteen weeks, though, I slowly realized what it was. There was a tiny person in there that wasn't able to choose whether it would live the next day or not. That baby was floating around, growing bigger and stronger each day, and looking to me to meet its basic needs for survival. It didn't ask to be here, so who was I to take away an innocent life? Tears filled my eyes and my heart ached with overwhelming emotions.

There were times when my son was younger that I would place him on a countertop and hold out my arms. He would get a huge smile on his face and leap into my waiting arms with no fear that I would catch him. There was no doubt in his young trusting mind that I would keep him from falling and injuring himself on the ground beneath. I suddenly saw this picture in my vision and heard something deep down in my spirit say, *"Jump."* My spirit was stirred, and despite all of the ways that my mind tried to convince me otherwise, my heart overruled. I decided right then to take a leap of faith, and trust in a God that I felt deep in my soul was waiting, with loving arms outstretched.

My mind was suddenly made up. I called and cancelled my abortion appointment and I chose life for my unborn baby and a new life for myself. I packed our things, said a silent prayer for guidance, and moved in with the Hansons that very weekend.

~~~~~~~

When Israel was freed from slavery in Egypt, although they were at first relieved, soon they began to grumble and complain. Even though they had become free, they brought a "slave mentality' with them.

After a while, they didn't even appreciate freedom from release of bondage; they just saw it as another form of slavery. Therefore, they walked around lost for forty years and never walked into the promises of God because of their attitudes. Sometimes we don't even realize when we are actually being *set free*. We begin to *miss* the former yoke of bondage and often seek to return to it. I wasn't sure I was fully ready to give up TV, secular music, and sleepovers with my boyfriend. As I settled in, it seemed so quiet and boring there. *What would I do all day?* I thought bitterly. What I didn't realize was that pretty soon my mind would become freed from distraction and chaos and mindsets that I didn't even realize were keeping me from the best that God had for me and my children. But not yet—in my view, my life was good just as it was.

When I originally went to live with this Christian family, the Hansons in Costa Mesa, California, although I was relieved and grateful to have a place to stay, I also was resentful of having rules and regulations imposed upon me at a time when I was a mother and felt as if I was "grown and independent." In the beginning, because I hadn't grown up seeing solid, trustworthy relationships, I looked at the family with mistrust and doubt. It was hard for me to believe that there were people out there who would do something so unselfishly, without plans to receive something out of it for themselves. I didn't know whether they truly cared for me or were just putting on a show.

At times I even felt depressed. I felt I had no one to talk to. I was out of my element and often felt out of place in this "happy-go-lucky" family. I felt like Arnold on the TV series *Different Strokes*. When I observed the family singing songs while the wife played guitar, baked bread, and taught her children the Bible, at first all I could think in my mind was "*Whatchu talkin 'bout, Willis?*" I had no frame of reference from which to pull these people and their picture-perfect life.

"Help! I'm in Brady Bunch hell!" I often said to my boyfriend, who thought it was hilarious. I stayed in my room, secluded for the first few weeks, but soon, slowly, over months, I warmed up to the family. They made me feel at home, and my son got along pretty well with their children. I helped the wife cook meals that we placed at the table and ate together when her husband came home. She took me along grocery shopping, taught me how to make homemade bread, and I watched her keep to a strict family budget and saw how she kept her home fairly neat and orderly. David was very friendly and seemed to enjoy spending time with his family. I mostly watched everything they did—not looking for them to do wrong, but because I was so surprised that families like this existed.

The relationship between them was indescribable. Although Karen was more vocal and outgoing, she sweetly and humbly allowed David to be in charge. She had a great sense of humor, and she thought I was the funniest person ever, so we laughed a lot. David was a soft-spoken man, but I watched as he often talked to her in detail about any plans he was considering, consulted with Karen for suggestions, and in the end, his decision stood. Although he was a leader, he led with love, respect, and confidence. Because of this, her submission was willing and out of mutual respect. They were affectionate with each other, and mannerly toward me and each other. This blew my mind, because most relationships I'd seen needed police intervention on a regular basis.

They didn't even curse! Growing up, profanity was something I heard all day, every day. My dad had the vocabulary of Eddie Murphy in *Raw* and all of our movies, music, and family members spoke this way. My mother didn't curse a lot, except when she got mad, but I had picked up that habit and at the time, I talked just like my dad. I also had natural comedic timing and a sense of humor, much like my entire family. I was a rap fan as well; Easy E and NWA were my favorite artists. I knew every word to their albums from memory, and my friends and I often screamed them out at school. In this home, though, I watched my tongue and didn't want to offend anyone. It was a huge transition, and one that I often struggled with initially.

The two pretty little blonde Hanson girls could be a handful at times. Corrine was active and smiling and asked questions constantly, and Micah was very temperamental. She screamed and cried mercilessly, oftentimes for no reason. From what I remember, she cried more than she didn't, and I would get so exhausted from just hearing it that I would grab my son and head to my room. Micah was deep into the "terrible twos" and her favorite word was "NOOOO!" And we typically heard it all day long. She often gave Karen the blues, but Karen kept herself very calm and loving, at times when I myself would have snapped. Being young, I had low tolerance for crying and misbehavior. I would hit baby Gerald on his legs or hands if he had a fit and think nothing of it. My dad had always taught me that if you yelled NO! sharply and hit the child really hard on the hand, they would learn quickly. When you do it about five times in a row, it's like Pavlov's dogs; the next time you sharply yell NO! they jerk their hand back and automatically run off without even needing the hit. Worked like a charm.

However, Karen wanted to discourage me from hitting and had me read several parenting books on discipline. The funny thing is, from what I learned in the book, when you tell them something once and they don't listen, you spank them. I laughingly showed Karen, and in my opinion, it actually served to solidify my position.

~~~~~~~

Church was interesting, to say the least. It was called Calvary Chapel Costa Mesa. This church was pretty much all "white," and very calm and mellow in its praise and worship. We went and took the kids, dropping them off at the baby childcare room. I hadn't had much church experience, except I loved Miss White's church as a kid and my Maranatha teen youth group left great memories, so I quickly got used to it. It wasn't as upbeat and emotional as the African American churches I remembered, but the lessons were still quietly powerful, and enlightening. We read out of hymnals and everything was rather soothing, and the pastor was soft voiced. It was so soothing, in fact, that I often fell straight asleep during the services. I felt like what he was saying was nice and all, but I was also tired, with a one-year-old child and being pregnant. This was my time of rest. We went Sunday mornings, and Wednesday night for Bible study. Karen and David never said much about me sleeping in church. They were very patient and kind as to my condition.

I slowly got into a routine. I would wake up, get dressed (because I wasn't allowed to walk around the house in my pajamas), and get little Gerald bathed and groomed. He was a sharp little kid, and wore boots, jeans, sweaters, and turtlenecks at all times. I always had him matching, and he looked great in blue because it matched his eyes. Then we would eat breakfast with Karen and the kids (David often left early) and clean up afterward. Then Karen would put on a praise tape/video for the kids and start handling her day while I puttered about, chasing after little Gerald who was always a handful.

Early afternoons, we would load the kids in a little red wagon and go for walks up and around the neighborhoods, or do whatever shopping was to be done that day. Afterward, we came back, ate lunch, and the kids might play outside for a short time more, then everyone, including me, went down for a nap; I was grateful because I was always tired. Then we would wake up, prepare dinner, set the table, and David would arrive soon, at which time we would eat together, share Karen's stories from the day, and talk about David's day as well. When dinner was over we'd clean up and then Karen would often sing with her guitar. Next it was upstairs with the kids for their baths and Bible study, while I went to my room to read or make a call to my boyfriend, then prepare my son for bed. Karen had assigned me to read a parenting book (as was part of my housing requirement), and I would often read that at night, or whatever other book I had handy, which I didn't mind, being an avid reader anyway. These were daily rituals that were not often interrupted, except on church days. Then we'd have dinner earlier, go to church, come home, and prepare for bed. Most times, we were all in bed by 9 p.m. Then the next day we'd do it all over again.

In the beginning, I must admit, I was bored out of my mind. Even the food was obscenely healthy. Homemade breads, fruits, yogurts, and square meals three times a day. I loved to eat so I didn't complain, but there was never the "soul food," unhealthy foods, fast foods, sugared candies, and "kool-aids" I grew up with and enjoyed as part of a normal diet. White grape juice was the most "risqué" we got around there. It seemed that everything required adjustment for me during this time.

In the backyard of their home were lots of play things—a sand box and a huge playground constructed for the kids to climb on. Often, while the children played outside, we fixed lunch as Karen watched them through the kitchen windows and the sliding door, which directly connected to the backyard. I was a stickler about keeping little G neat and clean, and in the beginning I would not allow him outside to play with the girls. I was pretty protective over him since he was all I had, and I rarely had any help. I didn't ever want him dirty, and Karen would often laugh about that. "He's a baby, let him play! Nothing wrong with letting them get dirty—they wash off," she would plead, smiling. Her children were often without shoes, with chubby dirty cheeks and into making mud-pies and playing with tree branches. I winced. "No, he's fine," I would say, keeping him tightly on my lap. But as we spent more time there, little G made it clear he wanted to venture and play, and eventually I pulled his little boots and socks off and let him run free. He had a blast. At first I chased after him, wiping him down and holding his hand, but after a while I settled into a lawn chair next to Karen and let him roam. After that, I even relaxed on his wardrobe and let him wear "play clothes" and play outside. Lo and behold, Karen was right...it didn't hurt him. He actually enjoyed and began to look forward to outside time.

~~~~~~~

Karen and I grew closer over time and talked a lot. I was always an extremely talkative person growing up, and asked questions like crazy. My family members always got exhausted telling me a simple story because I wanted so many details! I literally wanted and still want to create a visual picture when I'm hearing about something, so I will make a person back up in their story, start from the beginning, and give small details, such as weather and facial expressions. This can turn a five-minute story into thirty minutes easily. "Oh, Lord, here we go. I have to break it down for Miss Twenty Questions," my family would sigh in frustration. They constantly said I would one day either be a lawyer or a journalist because of my attention to detail and great memory for facts and events.

But Karen never minded feeding my curious nature. She loved to talk as well, so we were a great fit and both would chatter on and on. We became each other's friend during that time, and to me it seemed we were closer than any current friends I already had. She told me the background story of her relationship with David, and how she was once a headstrong young cheerleader and went through a rebellious phase, and how they once lived in a trailer like hippies, and how their first house was so small you could barely walk past one another in the kitchen. I told her all about my family stories, how Gerald and I first met, the trials we endured, and how I had come to arrive at the place I was. We talked many hours daily as we watched and cared for the children, sometimes late into the night after everyone else had gone to bed.

I was never told that I had to believe in God, pressured to listen to or to agree with their views, and they never pointed out my faults or shortcomings; they just modeled God with their lives. Eventually, seeing the light around them and their family, I wanted to know more about the God they served…on my own. In the book of Peter 3:1, wives are told, *Be submissive to your own husbands so that even if any of them are disobedient to the word, they may be won without a word by the behavior of their wives.* In other words, if someone in your circle is unsaved, you don't have to preach, holler, guilt, nag, or bash someone over the head with God's Word for them to repent of their ways and receive Christ. From my viewpoint—a young unsaved girl who was just really learning about God—none of those methods would have had a positive effect on me. As a matter of fact, they would only have served to stir up rebellion in me that eventually would have led me to seek the nearest exit strategy. Instead, the Bible says that when it comes to witnessing, often no words are even necessary—just live the life, and others (including a wayward spouse) will eventually be won over by your godly, loving conduct. All I knew at the time was that after a few weeks living with Karen and David Hanson, that old hunger in me for God was refueled and I was curious to learn more.

CHAPTER 6

From Rebellion to Love

I THINK THE REASON why the movie *Annie* was one of my favorites as a child is because it's the story of an orphan who was desperately seeking her missing parents, hoping against hope that they would find and love her again, and instead she found love and a new unconventional family in unexpected places. Although both of my parents were alive and well, I felt very much like a lost orphan in my own life, seeking love and acceptance and never quite feeling that void was being filled. God sees our lack and what is missing when we are growing up, and will provide that in our lives if we allow Him to. It says in Psalms 68:5 that He desires to be a *"father of the fatherless."* Growing up, I had many needs that I didn't even know I had, but God knew. I didn't know it at the time, but God was teaching me about love and marriage, commitment and family, and roles and responsibility, all while bringing me into a gradual awareness of who He really is. Being that I had had few experiences with God and always had a desire to learn more, I soaked it up like a sponge, watching everything that this family did, and said.

I watched how they communicated with each other with mutual respect, how they put time and energy into their children, and how peaceful and relaxing the environment was. I didn't even know before this that I had been internally stressed. Although I was only a teen, I had experienced a lot and grew up at a young age. In the beginning, all I wanted to do was sleep, and it seemed I finally caught up on years of sleep within a few weeks.

Not being able to watch TV and listen to secular music was at first pretty hard for me. Music was something that was always playing in either of my parents' homes from speakers all day long. I knew the words to all songs, from oldies R & B to the latest rap lyrics. I was pretty confident at the time that these lyrics had no negative effect on me. In my mind, it was all just entertainment and fun. As I said before, parties and clubs were a normal part of life when I was growing up. So initially with the Hansons I had to really adjust, and I felt like I was going through serious withdrawals. But eventually, it felt like a "cleansing" experience, in that the longer I went without listening and watching, the less I ended up missing it. I learned the words to the kids' praise tapes that Karen played through the house, and even bought myself a couple of contemporary Christian CDs from artists like Crystal Lewis, who performed at the church often and had an R&B soulful appeal to her. I discovered that there was Christian rap as well, and I even bought Gerald a CD or two. Some of these artists seemed talented and still fed my need for music—the style I liked—but didn't inspire the same violent thoughts and lustful emotions that secular rap and R&B did.

Slowly, I adapted to the daily routines and found a new "project" to undertake: I decided to read and study the entire Bible. I had heard of people reading the Bible from cover to cover and I figured that there was no better time to tackle it. If I was going to learn about something, I wanted to know if it was even true or not. The length of the Bible did not daunt me. I had read large books before and wasn't at all intimidated. I loved to read. Besides, I had nothing but time on my hands.

I subscribed to the Christian Research Institute, which sends free information on all religions and how they differ from Christianity. I was interested in Christianity, but wanted to know why this Christian religion was even one I should consider. I felt that I needed to know more. I even got info on the backgrounds of other religions, everything from Jehovah's Witnesses, and Mormons, Muslims, and Buddhists, and others, and learned how they compared to Christianity. I then read the entire Bible for myself. I didn't want to depend on a pastor to translate for me; I wanted to know that I'd seen it with my own eyes. I learned that sometimes people "quoted" things that were nowhere in the Bible. And many times people twisted things that God said to fit their own selfish interests, such as was the case with slavery. The problem I had, though, was that when I read the King James Bible, however, I didn't understand it, and eventually found myself either falling asleep or not able to get the full meaning. So Karen gave me a Life Application Bible, and I got the idea to set both of those books on my desk side by side (I didn't know about a Parallel Bible at this time, where the two translations are already made into one book) because although I loved the Life Application translation, I still wanted to know if it lined up with the original. So, first, starting with Genesis, I read the King James Version, and then I would look over and use my other Bible to translate the meaning. It was a great learning experience and it was during this time when, along with going to church twice a week, I felt something growing, shifting, and changing inside of me. It was as if I was emptying the "old stuff" out and pouring some new stuff in. Little did I know at the time, but it was all preparation for my future.

And I was starting to feel so…different. The first sign: about a month after I moved in, Gerald came to pick up little Gerald and me a couple of times. He had bought a bright red two-seater Z-28, which I didn't understand because there was no room for the three of us (soon to be four), but back then there were no mandatory seatbelt laws so we packed up and, baby in lap, we were off to visit friends and family. Gerald met Karen and David and immediately took to them. At the time, he claimed not to like "white people," but with their disarming smiles and sweet temperament, it would have been hard for even the most militant Black Panther not to like them right away.

As we got into the car, Karen watched and helped me get buckled in, and I remember that she leaned over and said to Gerald in a very motherly way, "Be very careful. You have precious cargo here." And that always made me feel warm inside, as if I had a concerned mother hen. She always seemed as if she was hesitant to let us go off, and ever concerned for my well-being. I was starting to like and appreciate that.

On the road, Gerald, an avid Tupac Shakur fan, would turn on the radio dial, and immediately profanity would fill the air. Although I had been raised up listening to the words and even had used them myself in the past, after a month living in the Hanson home those words shocked and appalled me. I covered my son's ears and my mouth flew open. "Oh my God! Turn that off!" I yelled.

Gerald looked at me as if I was crazy, but he complied. For a moment, I was shocked…that I was shocked. I couldn't believe how bad the music sounded to me now. It was as if I had never heard the words before. I think that was the first time I really noticed I was no longer the same girl who went into that house thirty days earlier. Profanity was no longer something that was acceptable to me. Something about it no longer seemed "right." I explained it to Gerald, but he didn't seem too eager to give up his listening habits, nor did he really see my point. But he respected me enough not to play it again in my presence. The rest of that day we drove around, hung out, met with Gerald's family members, and spent quality time together, but my curfew was 11 p.m., and to be honest, I couldn't wait to get back to the house, where I was starting to feel more and more at home.

~~~~~~~

I had some cash saved up from past jobs in an old savings account, and I also applied for and received government assistance. It helped with bottles, clothes, and other baby supplies. Gerald worked at a grocery store for a while and would help with diapers and milk. Sometime during the first month that I lived with the Hansons, a lady I knew told me she was moving out of state and was selling her old car for $800. It was a Volkswagen Beetle, a cute car at a great deal. It wasn't painted but was beige with primer. It ran great, and I loved it.

I gathered a few hundred and got the rest from my mom to get the car. There were several problems though: I still hadn't gotten a license (because my dad had refused to teach me to drive when I lived with him), and this car was a stick shift. Nevertheless, I was still excited at the prospect of having a car to call my own. I bought it, signed the title, and was overjoyed. I had a car! I did my happy dance as I bought cleaning supplies, washed the car inside and out, and even sat in it for hours listening to the radio, cleaning, and decorating. I added furry lambskin seat covers and dangled charms from the rearview mirror. I was ready to go!

But my excitement didn't last long. Karen and David sat me down and, to my dismay, laid down the *car rules*. Before I could drive anywhere, they explained, I needed to have a driver's license and car insurance. "It's the law," they said. That let all the hot air right out of my balloon. Inside I was fuming. These weren't my parents—who are they to tell me what I can do with a car I bought? So for weeks and weeks, I left my car in the driveway and continued to ride everywhere with them in the family van. And when alone, I sat in the window of my bedroom and stared achingly out at my car, knowing it was mine and longing for the day when I would actually drive it. It felt like torture to me.

Finding insurance wasn't as hard as I thought. Although I was young and inexperienced, I found a generic company overseas that offered me a decent rate, so I got that out of the way. I scheduled my written exam and studied books given out at the DMV. Gerald took me for a few test runs in his Z so I could learn the stick shift, but he quickly grew impatient and scared that I was tearing up his transmission. He would throw me out of the driver's seat after about fifteen stressful minutes; I felt hopeless. How would I get my license if I couldn't drive? I eventually passed the written test so I knew all the rules of the road, but I still needed real life behind-the-wheel lessons.

Karen, seeing my distress, finally agreed to help me learn to drive a stick shift. We took a few days over the weekend when David was home so that he could watch the kids.

The streets of Costa Mesa where we lived are much like San Francisco. They're made up of very high hills and deep slopes that sometimes seem almost like a roller coaster. Some streets seemed to point straight up into the air. Once I got behind the wheel, Karen showed me that you had to really coordinate pressing the gas and releasing the clutch pedal at such a time so that there wasn't a horrible jerk, which would make the car shut off, or even worse, do a backwards roll, which could potentially cause an accident. Both of these things were my greatest fears on those hills! Driving and staying in the lanes was easy enough, but going into traffic made my heart pound and hands sweat. I tried to stop as little as possible, and with all the panicked yells and fast turns, Karen and I laughed and screamed as I jerkily took corners and hesitantly stopped at lights, often unable to start up again. People behind me constantly honked, and sometimes I was so overwhelmed and slow that I had to flag them to just go around me.

"I can't do this!" I would scream, always the drama queen.

"Breathe, relax, you can do it!!" she would tell me, laughing at my expressions until her sides hurt.

At one point, we came to a four-way stop sign. Cars were at each stop sign—this was a big moment for me. I knew from studying my manual that the person to my right went first, but it just so happened that I was the person to everyone's right and had gotten there first, so it was on me. The scariest part was that I was also angled up a hill, with a car now pulling up behind me. As I released the brakes, I felt the car rolling backward as I tried to change gears and quickly press the gas, and I kept throwing back on the brakes. I was so scared of hitting the car waiting behind me that I froze up. But Karen started to pray and kept telling me that I could do it. After three tries and a near miss, I was able to focus, coordinate my feet, and listen to the sounds enough to feel and hear when it was done just right…and propel the car forward. It was a sweet victory to me, and we "high fived" ourselves, laughing. "Yay, God is good!" she would yell, cheering me on. After that, it was no longer a problem for me to do. It took that big moment of pressure from all sides for me to learn how to get it right.

Our relationship with God is often like that. Sometimes we feel there are obstacles on all sides while we are trying to grow, learn, and change. It may seem too challenging and that we want to give up. But if we just focus on the task at hand and don't allow the voices in our head to win, we can eventually make that transition. It takes patience, determination, and the ability to listen and wait for the right moment. I learned so many lessons that day and developed a new confidence in my own ability.

After about a week of practice, I got the hang of merging my written knowledge of the road into actual application. I learned coordination with mirrors, how to tell if someone was in your blind spot, and to constantly be on watch for dangers as well as to pay attention to my hands and feet at the same time. I learned to make easy, gentle stops, downshift on the turns, and even began to successfully Parallel Park. I felt so accomplished! Learning how to drive is hard enough, but learning on a stick shift, on rollercoaster roads—that takes work. And amazingly, Karen stayed patient and humorous the whole time. She never yelled or lost her patience, although I am sure she saw her life flash before her eyes many times over!

Finally the time came to take my scheduled driver's exam. Before they would give the test, they wanted to make sure everything worked: lights, turn signal, and horn. For some reason, at that moment the horn wouldn't work. I tried several times, and just as they were getting ready to tell me I had to reschedule, I prayed myself, and Karen prayed with me, and the horn blew loudly. I was so grateful. I was starting to feel like she had some sort of magical direct line to God Himself.

It was time for my test. I was nervous, but I did everything perfectly and passed the road test with flying colors. My reward was my brand new, certified driver's license! Karen and David both congratulated me and made me feel very special. I started to feel that independence was within reach for me. Finally I would go out on my own… in my own car.

On my first ventures out in my own car, I made a short few runs to the store and back, but the problem wasn't with my technical driving skills—it was that I was horrible with directions. If I could find my way to my destination, I couldn't quite get back from wherever I went. Directions for me had to be written out, both GOING and COMING BACK, or I would get lost. Karen thought that was so funny.

Streets and turns confused me, and I had never been one to pay attention in the past when I was a passenger. I just never cared to learn. So when I took trips to the store or mall, Karen wrote down directions there and, at my request, turned the paper over and wrote return directions. This may seem funny, but I am still bad at this: mind you, this was before Mapquest and Google Navigation, which help me greatly now!

My biggest challenge came the day I decided to take lil' Gerald out visiting. My goal was to visit my dad who lived about thirty minutes away. I called and got directions from my dad, packed up my son and got on the road, leaving about 10 a.m. Thirty minutes turned into one hour. I don't know if I missed an exit or took a wrong freeway, but I stopped at several gas stations asking directions. Everyone gave me different directions, and it seemed I travelled one road five or six times; they all looked alike to me. There were no cell phones so when I called my dad from a phone booth, he wouldn't answer as he often didn't when he didn't recognize the number on caller ID. So hour after hour went by with me driving around blindly. After four hours, I was extremely frustrated and my car started smoking out of nowhere. It was getting dark...I was angry, tired, and scared. Lil' G slept the whole time so he didn't seem to mind the drive. But I didn't know what was wrong with the car and felt like I had failed my first attempt at independence. I finally gave up and called Karen and David from a gas station off the highway in the middle of nowhere. They were kind enough to drive out to get me, an hour away from home, and I sadly followed them back. Turns out they were worried about me anyway, not having heard from me for hours. It was my first and last attempt to travel long distance in my car.

Since I didn't go out much, and Gerald was busy with school and work, I had plenty of time during the day to spend in the Word. As I read my Bible, I started having questions about God. I wanted to know why certain things happened the way they did. I held certain beliefs that were based on my upbringing, and I was starting to be open to the fact that they may not have been right. Since I was young, I always wanted a husband, family, and kids, and the paths I had taken and the one I was now on didn't seem to lead to success in those areas. Karen sat up with me late into the evening answering my questions and discussing scriptures with me. Sometimes they hosted fellowship Bible studies at the house, and I watched as all these sweet, loving people came over, read and discussed the Word.

Many of them were families with teens, and I was blown away by how godly these teenagers were, how gently they spoke, how considerate and loving they were toward their parents, and vice versa. Those young girls had a glow I had never seen! Their friends embraced me as if I was another daughter, a friend—and truth be told, I was starting to feel like one. I went everywhere they went, and we bonded. Even my interactions with Gerald were different. We didn't argue, and I was much more patient and kind. Through reading scripture, I started to feel closer to God and wanted to have Him more in my life.

I developed my own personal prayer routine. I also was still reading the Bible each day. I wrote letters to Gerald about my feelings, and my hopes for him to be a loving responsible father, which is something he himself didn't have. I wrote that hopefully we would one day be a true family. For the first time, I started to want for myself what I saw in the Hanson household. I wanted that type of relationship, not the fighting and chaos I'd seen growing up. I wanted my children to be raised with love and caring, and in an environment of security and peace. From what I was seeing, having God as the head and living a lifestyle committed to serving Him, was one of the crucial keys to obtaining this.

~~~~~~~

One day Karen told me she was going to a meeting, and she wanted me to go with her. It was early evening and I assumed it was another form of Bible study. We went into a rec center type building and I saw lots of people seated, and someone standing at a podium telling their story, and everyone was clapping and encouraging one another. I had grown accustomed to seeing people talking about God, crying, and ministering to each other, so at first I assumed this was nothing new, but quickly I noticed something was different. These people were not saved, and not all of them talked about God. They talked about overcoming drugs and addictions, and other failures they were enduring. This piqued my interest. As each person rose to tell their story and I looked at the flyers on the walls, I realized this was an Alcoholics Anonymous meeting. The people discussed their steps to change, and there were some pretty sad stories. The thing I noticed though was that each person got love and support from the group to continue on, as well as praised for each day that they were clean and sober. Some of those people came once a day, some once a week, and others, monthly or less. It all depended on what they needed, and the pressures that they were feeling.

Soon, Karen went forward to take the podium. Because she was so sweet and kind, I assumed they had asked her to come guest speak, but as I listened I was again surprised. She wasn't a speaker so her nervousness was evident.

"My name is Karen Hanson, and I am an alcoholic," she stated to applause.

She told a story of how she was promiscuous, and involved in a rebellious lifestyle. She said she was on a downward spiral, and turned to alcohol in an attempt to cover her pain from her past. She testified on how God brought her out. Her story was different in the way that she ministered the absolute love and forgiveness of God, even over the twelve steps they promoted in the program brochures. Some were moved to tears, others seemed uncomfortable. She had never told me these things, so I was blown away. Never in a million years did I imagine her as being anything besides a wholesome upright Christian girl all her life. But come to find out, she had been a wild child, and an alcoholic. This was a wakeup call to me that not everyone had to be perfect for God to touch their lives.

Previously when I was introduced to all these people in Karen and David's circle, and all these sweet, innocent teens, often I had felt inadequate and insecure because I felt like I couldn't measure up somehow. In a way, I had felt as if maybe they were better than me and had more opportunities than I did to be successful. They never made me feel this way; it was my own feeling based on the contrast I saw in my own life. But when I went to this meeting with Karen and saw that she once had insecurities, hurts, pain, and shortcomings that she continued to work every day to overcome, I felt a connection to her like never before.

I'm not sure what made her go to that meeting that night. Maybe she was feeling stressed, and tempted to drink; I will never know. All I know is that it was a major shift in my beliefs about having to be "perfect" for God to accept me. Karen's past struggles were worse than my own, and she had overcome, and found love and healing through God, and her marriage and family. After the meeting I hugged her, and told her what a great job she had done.

It was then that I knew: through her love, support, encouragement, talks, prayers, lessons, and examples, I had started to fall in love—not only with them, but with the God they represented. And while I was choosing Him, I didn't even realize that He had already had His hands on and chosen me, so many years earlier.

You did not choose me, but I chose you and appointed you to go and bear fruit—fruit that will last. ~John 15:16

CHAPTER 7

Born Again

JESUS IS A PERFECT GENTLEMAN. He waits while we make our choices in life. While we endure heartache, pain, and trials...He waits. He never forces his way in. He says: *"Behold, I stand at the door and knock. If anyone hears my voice and opens the door, I will come in to him and eat with him, and he with me"* (Rev 3:20). In other words, He must be *invited* into our hearts. He gives us the choice whether or not to have a relationship with Him, as part of the gift of our free will. In life, every choice you make determines the path your life will eventually take—even the ones that seem minor, and inconsequential.

By deciding to keep my baby, and move in with the Hansons, I was unknowingly deciding to journey in a different direction for myself, and my descendants. As I read my Bible daily, I discovered that God loved me, and wanted to have a *relationship* with me, which I discovered is different than a *religion*, in that there is no way you can "earn" it. I also knew in my heart that God had sent Jesus to die on the cross, and that in order to get salvation; I needed to be born again. How did I know this, even though I wasn't raised to believe this, and with all of the other religions I'd experienced? I have no idea, but I just *knew*. I felt in my heart that God was leading me toward this revelation. However, initially, I was not quite prepared to make that big of a step, because, honestly, I wasn't sure if I would be missing out on things. I also knew that one of the things I would need to "give up" if I became saved was premarital sex, and I didn't know how a relationship with Gerald would last if I did that.

As my belly grew, summer moved quickly into sweltering heat. I read the book *What to Expect When You're Expecting* and learned all about pregnancy, birth, and delivery. The first time, I had been really naïve during my pregnancy, so I wanted to be more prepared this time around. Once the four and a half months of nausea had passed, and I was more actively feeling the tiny kicks of the baby, I felt better and decided to enjoy the rest of my pregnancy. I had a boy already, so secretly I wanted a girl. I wanted someone I could dress in frilly dresses, and do her hair. Little Gerald was a "pretty" boy who people always assumed was a girl whenever I took him out. He was blue eyed (genes inherited from my dad) with blondish hair that I kept in a silky ponytail. But that was the only thing feminine about him. Otherwise, he was all one-hundred percent active boy! He ran around being rough, tumbling, and tearing up things all day long. Gerald's brothers and nephews were all very rough with him, and when little G went there to visit; he would come back out of control, and hyper for at least two days. He earned the nickname "Monster" back then, which stayed with him until this very day. Sometimes I didn't know what to do with him and became frustrated easily, which Karen usually helped me with.

I didn't go to my first doctor's appointment till I was five months pregnant, and because of that, the doctor was pretty rude. I didn't explain to him that I hadn't been sure I would keep the baby until that point, but they still treated me like an ignorant teenager. Gerald was in and out of town with school, and I often went to appointments alone, or with Karen. They scheduled my ultrasound and told me since I was further along, I should definitely be able to find out the sex if I wanted to know. With my first baby, I hadn't; I wanted it to be a surprise. But with this baby, I couldn't wait. The ultrasound would be in a few weeks.

As the days passed and my stomach grew, I started coming more out of my shell and enjoying life with the Hansons, now tolerating their rules and lifestyle without complaint. Karen had a little radio that she used to play in the kitchen of her home, and she listened to *Focus on the Family* daily, as well as Christian music. One day while she was in the backyard with the kids, I was sitting in the kitchen getting something to drink, when I heard an interview with my favorite Christian artist at that time, Crystal Lewis. She had written a new song and they were featuring it on the show. She explained that she had written it herself directly to Jesus in honor of his great sacrifice on the cross, and it meant a lot to her. Something made me come closer to the radio and lean in.

The words to the song went like this:

"I'll never know why, why you did what you did…
You didn't have to die…
But you did
You hung on the cross, so that I wouldn't be lost…
You took my place, now you're pleading my case…
Didn't have to do it…
Oh, but I'm glad you did."

As I listened to the beautiful music and words, I became deeply moved with emotion. I thought about the scriptures I had read, detailing the painful crucifixion of Christ, as well as recently watching the Easter program on the crucifixion. I thought about how he took all my sins upon Himself, and suffered so that I could live, and how He didn't have to do it, but did it anyway out of love. I also thought of how He never forced his way into my life, but patiently waited for me to choose to love Him in return.

Listening to that song, I broke down right there in that kitchen! It seemed to hit me all at once that I had a Savior, and that God loved *me* enough to send His son to die for me. The lessons I'd learned over the past couple of months, and the talks and church visits were finally reaching my heart, and making me want to change. I knew I wanted God in my life. I knew what being saved was, but up until that point I had never really accepted the gift of salvation. That night, I talked to Karen about it and what it entailed and she gave me all the information.

Every week at church, I had also seen the verbal invitations at the end of each service that invited people to come forward to join the church and get saved. When I was younger, I was taken backstage at Miss White's church and they tried to teach me to "speak in tongues," but it didn't feel genuine, and I was embarrassed more than anything. It made me afraid to go into that back room again, not knowing if I would be able to do what they asked of me. But Karen just told me that going forward to receive any gift of the spirit was a matter of acceptance, and required a verbal confirmation of that acceptance, as well as getting information about what it means, and being prayed over. I didn't tell her at that point that I was thinking about joining the church, but it was good to get some answers I felt comfortable with.

~~~~~~

Born Again

On Father's Day in 1992, Karen made David a nice breakfast and all of the kids told him happy Father's Day. I spoke to Gerald and wished him happy Father's Day, too, and while he made plans to see the baby on that day, I had made plans of my own…

I wanted to get saved.

That morning at church, I was nervous. *Could I go through with it? Would I be embarrassed? Would I feel different?* As the pastor wrapped up his sermon that morning, he ended the usual way: "*If anyone wants to make Jesus Christ the head of his life, please come forward and we will lead you in prayer.*"

Slowly I stood up and made my way, big belly and all, down to the front of the aisle. I felt that every eye was on me, and I continued on despite the butterflies (or kicks) I felt coming from within.

As I was led to the back room, a nice woman held my hand and told me that several steps were required for rebirth: admission of being a sinner, my need for Jesus, repentance of my sin—which meant not only forgiveness, but turning away from them—believing Christ died for my sins on the cross, and finally, receiving Jesus as my personal Lord and Savior. I agreed to all terms and made the confession.
That was it…I WAS *SAVED*!!

Becoming a Christian doesn't mean that you have got it all "together" and are now suddenly a perfect person from that day forward. Becoming a Christian to me meant realizing that I needed a savior in my life to lead, guide, and direct me. I realized that I wasn't capable of handling things on my own, and that I needed God to change me from the inside out. It is all about admitting your imperfections and allowing

God's sacrifice of His son to atone for your own sins, and accept His unconditional love, and forgiveness. I knew that over time I would possibly continue to make mistakes, and I didn't feel different all at once, but I knew that I was taking the first step in a lifelong journey of becoming more Christ like on a daily basis. And, at eighteen years old, I was ready now to take that journey, and be fully committed to it.

"...if you confess with your mouth, 'Jesus is Lord,' and believe in your heart that God raised him from the dead, you will be saved" (Romans 10:9).

Karen hugged me tightly as I told her my news later that day…she was *so* excited! She told me to write down the date because it was now my "spiritual birthday." And I needed to celebrate yearly so I should keep a record. Father's Day wasn't too easy to forget though.

"What a great gift to your Heavenly Father, to get born again on Father's Day!" she exclaimed. She always seemed so proud of me, that I could only smile and feel good about myself too. I'd also read in my Bible (Mark 16:16) that you needed to *"believe and be baptized"* so I asked her what baptism was, and why it was necessary. She told me that Jesus had it done prior to His ministry as an example to believers. She said it was done monthly at our church, and that it was an underwater "death" of the former man and a "rebirth" of the new spirit man. I asked her how long they hold you under. I wasn't trying to be drowned, and die literally. She laughed and assured me it was mere seconds. I marked the date on my calendar so that I could participate in the next water baptism.

When I saw Gerald later that day, I told him about getting saved, and he seemed to be happy about. After all, he had been raised in a church. Although it wasn't necessarily enforced in his home, nor was he living it, he still had those roots, and considered himself a Christian as well. He told me he had been baptized as a child. I also nervously told him my other news: I was now going to be committed to *celibacy until marriage*. My body was now the Lord's temple, I explained. I couldn't have sex until I was married. I explained that if he married me eventually, then that would be great, but if not we would be, from this day on, just great friends raising two children. I didn't feel as bad about the decision as I thought I would. I wanted to be better, to do better, than those before me, and it seemed that sex was behind many of the problems and misfortunes I saw around me and within our respective families.

Gerald stared at me in surprise. Although he was a professed Christian, premarital sex was common within their family, and household. He told me that he had never been told that you are NOT supposed to have sex before marriage as a Christian. As a matter of fact, his own self-proclaimed Christian mother had been previously living with a man who she wasn't married to, but had three kids with. When I had talked to Karen about all this, she assured me—without speaking against anyone—that according to scripture it wasn't right, and that God indeed speaks against it. Anyone who studied the Bible ought to know that, she said.

When I told Gerald, however, he acted like he was hearing it for the first time.

On the next couple of times we got together, he persistently tested my resolve, and tempted me greatly, but I held fast to my vow. The realization quickly hit him that I was serious. Within a week...he proposed.

CHAPTER 8

A Special Surprise

Trust in the Lord and do good; dwell in the land and enjoy safe pasture. Take delight in the Lord, and he will give you the desires of your heart. ~Psalm 37:4

GOD REALLY WANTS OUR LOVE, loyalty, and obedience. He also wants to see us happy, just as much as any good and responsible earthly father. He also desires to bless us through our obedience. It seems like one good thing after another started happening for me soon after this. For one, it seemed as if all of my prayers were being answered. One of the best things about being born again was the change in my relationship with Gerald. As I grew closer to God, it seemed that Gerald started to love and respect me more. It was almost as if he saw the light shining within me, and was impressed. We no longer had any of the fights about him being untrustworthy, because I was not accusatory, or suspicious. He treated me with much more respect, and seemed thrilled with the fact that I was now saved. After so long of not wanting to "rush things", he seemed to really want to get married all of a sudden. (Of course, the imposed celibacy also likely played a role in his new enthusiasm.)

Every week I invited him to church, and even an annual "Harvest Crusade" that our church had at the Anaheim stadium, in which thousands got born again. I always prayed when it came time for the benediction: I wanted him to accept Christ, too...but he refused every time and said that he wasn't ready. It disappointed me but I had to accept it. The hard part for me, was that I read in my Bible that you are not to be "unequally yoked," and when I announced the fact that we were getting married to Karen and David, I could tell that, although excited, they wanted me to be careful about committing to someone who now held different views than my own, although they didn't say much. They just continued to tell me to pray about it. I told them Gerald was raised in the church, so *technically* he was a Christian, and dismissed all my inner reservations because I wanted so badly to have the family I was seeing them have. I just prayed that eventually Gerald would come around.

We didn't have a lot of money, so I purchased my own engagement ring out of a catalog. In the picture that ring was beautiful! And it was only $39.95, which impressed me most. When they finally delivered it, it wasn't necessarily "gold" but more like "yellow." I was still proud to wear it as a way to show the public that I was more than your average teen mother—I was a wife to be. I still laugh thinking about that cloudy little diamond and the yellow band that turned my finger green soon after. When I showed Karen and David and explained to them how cubic zirconium was just LIKE diamonds (according to the ad), they smiled, and exclaimed how wonderful and real it looked for only $39.95. I'm sure when I went to my room later, they must have laid in bed and laughed until tears came down, about the poor sweet girl who ordered herself a fake gold, cubic zirconium engagement ring out of a mail order catalogue!

Because I didn't want to walk down the aisle pregnant, we decided to get married right after the baby was born. I wanted at least two weeks after the birth to heal somewhat before getting married. We decided on the date September 5th, 1992, a Saturday. My due date was August 25th, according to my prediction. The doctors had difficulty determining the date because they said that I was measuring small. One doctor told me that according to my measurements, my due date was October 4, and another even asked me if I smoked. These things worried me because I hadn't had any problems with lil G's pregnancy, and I knew the exact day I conceived. It was the day I came down from Georgia, in late November. I knew October 4 was way off, but hopefully the ultrasound would give them a better indication. I don't know why the baby measured small—I ate healthy and didn't have any bad habits. So I was anxious to get the correct due date and make sure things were okay with the baby. It's funny how even when you don't want a baby at first, you can become protective and concerned about it. This baby was not even half as active as little Gerald was when I was pregnant with him. He had constantly moved, exhausting me even all night long. This baby went so long without moving that sometimes I had to call a nurse. One day I didn't feel anything for a whole day, and I had to go in to the hospital. But while there the baby moved on its own, and they found a steady strong heartbeat. It surprised me that even in utero this baby was already so different.

Finally, the day came for my ultrasound. Karen drove me to my appointment, and I was instructed to drink eight glasses of water an hour beforehand. This made it so hard! Your bladder would fill up, and then you danced around until it was ultrasound time. I think with the more modern equipment these days, you don't have to drink the water, but back then it was necessary. When they finally called my name, I was so desperate to use the bathroom that they told me I could empty half my bladder upfront. I was about to burst. Minutes later I sat on the table as they measured everything and told me that the due date was indeed just as I had calculated, and the date of the

A Special Surprise

baby matched exactly what I knew to be true. I breathed a sigh of relief as they said the baby was measuring normal, all organs were present, and it appeared healthy.

They asked me if I wanted to know the sex, and I told them yes. As they looked further, they gave me the best news of all: *"It's a girl."*

I was so happy. For once in my life, I felt as if all of my dreams were really coming true. I would have a boy and a girl, marry Gerald, and life would be perfect. Once I walked out of the ultrasound room, Karen was there waiting at the van; she got out and met me.

"It's a girl!" I gushed, and I broke down in tears. Karen hugged me outside the doctor's office as I cried.

I had so many dreams all at once: I wanted this girl to have a relationship unlike my mother and me. I envisioned and wanted closeness, and lots of love. I imagined days, months, and years of talks, and friendship. I wanted to spoil her, and treat her like a little princess. I started praying over her, and talking to her right there in my womb from that moment. Most of all, I cried because I was so close to aborting her, and never having her in my life at all... when at this moment, she was the biggest reason for the radical change in my life. I fell in love with her deeply from that day forward, having never even yet seen her little face.

In my mind's eye, I imagined my little girl would have light hair and be semi-bald, with blue eyes as little Gerald had was when he was born, so soon I set out buying lots of headbands and hats. Every time I got money I bought frilly dresses and pretty shoes and blankets and bows and ribbons. I bought her a car seat and set it up in the back of my

Volkswagen and just stared at it, day after day, knowing she would be in it in a little over two months' time. I went about considering baby names: Candace, Ashley, Briana, and Shelby were my top choices. I had always had such a hard time with my name, so I wanted something simpler for my own daughter.

I wanted her to have the life I never had.

For her, I desired a life of happiness, with God at the forefront. I was confident that I would raise the first generation of Christians in our family. I had a special bond with little Gerald as well, but Big Gerald had always claimed him as "his son," and seemed possessed with teaching him "boyish" things, such as how to be rough, and how to dribble a basketball. With a girl, I knew I could teach her to be a little lady and some of the things my grandmother taught me, like manners and daintiness, and she could wear pretty dresses, and we could dress alike. I had never felt so blessed in all of my life.

I was having a *daughter*!

PART 3

A COVENANT DECISION

*And both that morning equally lay
In leaves no step had trodden black.
Oh, I marked the first for another day!
Yet knowing how way leads on to way
I doubted if I should ever come back.*

CHAPTER 9

A New Creation!

IN THE ROBERT FROST POEM, the traveler at one point realizes that once he took a particular path in life, although he intended on eventually returning and taking the other road, *"knowing how way leads on to way, I doubted if I should ever come back."* In other words, once you make certain decisions in life, you can't undo them. Life is like that. One choice leads to another choice, and so on, which is why it is so important to carefully consider all of your choices in advance and weigh your options before you act. Counting the cost is crucial!

Jesus himself spoke of weighing your decisions heavily before making them. He said, *"Suppose one of you wants to build a tower. Will he not first sit down and count the cost to see if he has enough money to complete it? For if he lays the foundation and is not able to finish it, everyone who sees it will ridicule him, saying, 'this fellow began to build and was not able to finish'"* (Luke 14:28-29).

Counting the cost. Part of making choices not only involves knowing all the options available to you, but also prayer, consulting wise counselors, and seeking the discernment of the Holy Spirit who lies within. Once you make a certain choice, you also must be ready and willing to accept the consequences of those choices, good or bad. Own them—they were yours to make! So many of us spend time blaming others, and pretending we have no control over things that happen in our lives. This may be true when we are younger, but once we are teens and adults, we begin making *conscious choices* that will affect our future lives, and generations that will come after us. The type of spouse we choose, the career path we take, the relationships we surround ourselves with, all impact the paths we take, in one way or another. And sometimes these things come with quite a heavy price. The question is: *are we willing to pay it?*

In deciding I wanted to follow Christ, I had to learn to walk in love, and forgiveness. I had to throw away all of my former habits, and attitudes. I had to stop participating in sinful actions that were not pleasing to God, and learn to do things differently. I also knew that I would also have to cut off former relationships that weren't healthy for me, and surround myself with godly people who wanted to help me with my spiritual growth. This was hard, because in my life, Karen and David were the only Christians I knew. But they helped me greatly, and I was *on fire*! I wanted to learn as much as possible and be ready to tell others about my faith. During the time that I lived with the Hansons, I didn't see much of my friends and family, and I didn't even tell people that I was pregnant. But once I became saved, and Gerald proposed, I notified my family and some friends, and also started to tell them about the changes within me. Of course, it was not always well received. My dad laughed, and criticized. My mother was disappointed that I wasn't going to finish school, and my friends wondered how long it would last. Although I felt isolated in my new faith, I stayed respectful, and was determined to live this new life one-hundred percent, and not give in to the temptations of going backward. I had chosen a new path, and I was determined to walk in it till the end.

A couple of weeks after I was born again, when I was seven months pregnant, the date for the water baptism rolled around. I was excited to discover that the baptism would be in the Huntington Beach waters, followed by a barbeque. It was hot, sunny, and the perfect day. I was in good spirits, and looked forward to making a dramatic transition. Karen and David were bringing their family along, and coming with me for support. They packed up the girls, Corrine and Micah, and we all headed down to the beach, which wasn't far from where we were living, maybe twenty minutes or so.

As we approached the waters and the spot where the baptism would take place, I noticed that there were high cliffs right above the spot where people were getting baptized, and there were what seemed like hundreds of people standing on them, lined up, either to be baptized, or watch and congratulate. It was a beautiful scene. As I stepped out of the car and the wind whipped our faces, I heard guitars playing and people singing. Seagulls flew overhead, and the sparkle of the sun on the waters made everything seem incandescent. Everyone was smiling, arms were raised in surrender, and the multi-cultural crowds were united as one, and peacefully moving toward the ocean in what seemed like slow motion. In the water about waist-deep, four pastors stood in a row, baptizing each person as they came forward. Of course, I watched the people as they were dipped into the water and noticed they were under for no more than three seconds, which was a relief to me, and eased my fear of drowning. Karen brought her camera, and they both told me how proud they were of me. The scene was something out of a movie. It was so peaceful, and the atmosphere was so loving. I was moved to tears.

Eventually I got in a line to await my turn, and noticed with excitement that the pastor who would baptize me was Raul Reese. This man had an amazing testimony. He was once a husband and father, who was once so stressed and overwhelmed that he sat in his living room with a shotgun, ready to kill his wife, kids, and then himself when they walked in the door. However, as he flipped through the channels, he landed on a Christian television show featuring our pastor, Chuck Smith, who was talking about the love of God, and forgiveness and mercy. Raul dropped to his knees in tears and got saved right in the middle of his living room floor—and needless to say, never went through with the violence. He joined the church and, after several years of service, became a pastor himself. He was an anointed speaker and later had a really large church of his own. Imagine—a testimony to the power of God reaching you even through the television!

As I approached Pastor Reese, I was nervous and excited all at once. He smiled at me and looked at my enormous belly—I would be getting a two-for-one!

"Hello!" he greeted me warmly. "Have you accepted Jesus Christ as the head of your life? "

"Yes!" I replied.

"Great!" He did a brief rundown of what baptism signified, as well as its history, which I already understood. "I baptize you in the name of the Father, the Son and the Holy Spirit," he said, leaning me back and pulling me under the cool ocean waters.

As I was under the water, all I could think about was how this baby inside of me was being baptized, too, and would be born into a life of service to God. I imagined my old self falling away and felt as if I was letting it go for good.

As he brought me up, I felt refreshed, renewed, and *released*! The cool breeze hit my face and I smiled a huge grin at Karen, who took a picture of me soaked from head to toe.

A new creation! No turning back now…

> *Therefore, if anyone is in Christ, he is a new creation. The old has passed away; behold, the new has come.* ~2 Corinthians 5:17

Once we commit our lives to Christ and allow him to be the head over our lives, we decide that we are now "dead" to sin. By being baptized, we leave our past in a watery grave and come up with a new heart, a new mind. Once we are dead, we no longer have a say in what happens to us. We have given over that right when we asked Jesus to take charge. We no longer even have a vote: *dead men don't vote*! Too many of us say that we are committed to Christ, yet we still hold on to old actions, habits, and ways that we can't seem to let go of. We find it hard to give control over to God, because we have grown accustomed to making all the decisions. What I learned was that my own decisions in the past had obviously taken me down a wrong path and were not very reliable.

By trusting in God and giving up that control, it was now out of my hands—and in His. Since I knew He loved me, and had my best interest in mind, I knew He wouldn't steer me wrong. He can see the beginning to the end, like watching a mouse in a maze. I was just wandering around, not knowing where I would end up. But He could see the big picture, and could guide me to freedom. I just had to stay attuned to His voice, and not allow distractions to cause me to get out of His will.

As the baptisms began winding up and dusk started to settle, people lit tiki torches along the coastline, set up lawn chairs and blankets, and started a few huge bonfires. Barbeque pits sent delicious smells into the air, and people sang, and smiled. Karen, David, the kids and I settled onto our blankets, and they pulled out hangers with marshmallows on them. Laughter, love, and peace filled the atmosphere. I imagined this was what heaven was like—people and angels loving God, singing, worshipping, and loving one another for eternity. I had never experienced this before, and it amazed me. All I could do was sit in awe and enjoy the scene. I helped little G roast a few marshmallows that we ate together. He was having a great time, too, which always made me happy.

"You are *glowing*!" David said to me. He wasn't much of a talker, but whenever he did talk with me, it was always encouraging and wise. I never heard negativity come out of his mouth, and it was nice to see that there were men like that in the world. He reminded me of King David, a man's after God's own heart, strong yet humble, and so very loving toward his family. I admired him.

Karen agreed. "Yes, that's the Holy Spirit!" she exclaimed, taking picture after picture.

I smiled and held my son tightly. As darkness descended, and the bonfires burned brightly, the sounds of the ocean in our ears, I felt filled up with love and gratitude.

I knew that one day this would all come to an end, but in my heart I dreaded that day. How would it be when I had to go back into the "real world," around my family, and friends?

I wondered if Gerald and I could ever be like these people. I could only pray that we could, but I wasn't really sure deep in my heart. I just wanted this moment to last forever.

But I knew deep down inside that it couldn't.

CHAPTER 10

The Birth

For I know the plans I have for you," declares the LORD, "plans to prosper you and not to harm you, plans to give you hope and a future. ~Jeremiah 29:11

BEFORE WE ARE EVER BORN, God has a destiny for us and a purpose for why He made us. Although we often make our own plans in life, it is imperative that we consult with God and make sure everything goes along with His will. If we fail to do this, we will often find ourselves frustrated and failing. Many times we get so caught up in doing things "our way" that we rarely take the time to seek wisdom from the Holy Spirit whom God has placed within us, and also to wait on a simple word of confirmation before we move forward. Often when making decisions, God will lead us toward certain paths, block others, and permit others. I am not sure whether or not the situation I was in was in God's perfect will for my life, but it seemed to be in His "permissive" will—in other words, He was permitting it to happen, but my initial life choices weren't His best. Maybe at some point in life I'd gotten off the path He'd destined for me to travel, but God was still with me, helping me achieve the plans He had for my life regardless of the path I chose. It just took more "shuffling things around" and a little bit longer to get it right.

Over the next couple of months, I planned for a wedding and a baby at the same time. It was a pretty exciting time for me, and I felt like God was really moving in my life. I was learning and growing in the Word daily, and my pregnancy was progressing in a healthy manner, although they still continued to say that my baby measured slightly small. Since I had already had one child, I was familiar with the birth and delivery process. I had no medications with my first baby and didn't really have any plans to do so this time either. I had never heard of epidurals and didn't even know there were ways to block pain completely, so I was prepared for the pain I would face. As I got larger and more uncomfortable, I slept more but continued to go places, and do things with the family. I read the Bible to the baby in my belly, and purchased many new Christian CDs (including my new favorite artist Crystal Lewis) and played them in my room day and night. Karen and I discussed a peaceful and calm birth environment to include music, prayer, and praise, which I thought sounded nice. My first son's birth was so stressful to me that I looked forward to a nice, relaxing birth. I had my overnight bag packed for the hospital, as well as all baby items I needed.

From what I read in my labor and delivery books, you were supposed to wait until your contractions were between four and five minutes apart before you went to the hospital, so I planned on a typical birth, but I didn't realize then that it would be anything BUT.

On the morning of August 22, I started experiencing contractions. By now I already knew what they meant. They went on most of the day and were starting off about fifteen minutes apart. I wasn't really nervous but I called Gerald and alerted him. I called the doctors, and since I had already pre-registered, they just informed me to wait until they were four minutes apart.

The Birth

The strange thing about these contractions was that they would range in time. One minute they would be fifteen minutes apart, the next five minutes, and sometimes one minute. This went on all day, and Gerald came over toward early evening. He was nervous yet excited. We decided that I needed to walk around to speed things up, so Gerald and I went on a stroll around the block. The pains came more often but still not on a set schedule. They were extremely painful though, and I recognized the feeling—I knew this was it! I called the doctor and they said it may be false labor, which I didn't think it felt like. They told me to drink water and see what happened. I downed two whole glasses ... and the pain went away. They told me I was possibly just dehydrated. Eventually it got late, and since nothing new was happening, Gerald went home.

The pains started again really aggressively, waking me up out of my sleep about one in the morning. I woke up Karen and told her, and proceeded to drink more water, which made me feel slightly better but didn't stop the contractions. I also lost my mucous plug (mothers will know what I mean by that) and felt like the time was coming. My contractions were sometimes ten minutes apart, sometimes three minutes apart, and I really just thought that maybe I needed to go in and get checked. Again I called Gerald, and he came and took me to the hospital. They put me in a gown, and we waited. I was still in a lot of pain. They checked me and told me I was not in labor. They said it was false labor, because I was only two centimeters dilated and not even close to being ready. They checked the baby and said it sounded good, and even said the head was down, and I was ready to go—but not today. I was surprised. It felt real and was extremely painful. So they gave me an IV and said again I was likely dehydrated. The pains slowed, and I got dressed, and went home disappointed about 2 a.m. I really wanted to see this baby!

Once I got home, the pains increased. I walked around, even tried to take a shower, tried to drink water, and nothing seemed to help. I was miserable. I had been in pain for twenty-four hours and was no closer to having the baby. About 4:30 a.m, I couldn't take it anymore. The contractions were suddenly two minutes apart, and I was willing to just go sit at the hospital and wait if that's what it took. Again I told Karen, who said she would drive me, and called Gerald, asking him to meet me there.

Although it was only three hours later when I got to the hospital, the doctor examined me and said I was almost FULLY DILATED! I guess it hadn't been so "false" after all. I couldn't believe it was already time. I got into my gown, and they attached a fetal monitor to me. Karen was excited. She had brought my cassette player and was praying with Gerald and me, and playing her praise music in the room. I was grateful for her presence, because Gerald was tired and sleeping in the corner (something that would be a habit with each one of our birth experiences). They had me do a few test pushes to start bringing the baby out. Another doctor came in to examine me about a half hour later, and I could tell she seemed concerned while she examined me. She said she noticed on the fetal monitor that the baby's heart rate was dropping with each contraction, which meant that the baby was in slight distress. She also kept reaching inside of me and looking confused, which was starting to worry me. She said it appeared also that the baby was not head down, but in breeched position. This concerned me, and I felt slightly fearful. *What did that mean?* I wondered, *did women normally deliver babies upside down?*

I found this strange, since three hours earlier they sent me home telling me that the baby was head down, and ready to go. I wondered if babies turned completely upside down in the last hours of pregnancy. She said not likely, but she asked the medical staff to bring in an ultrasound machine. The ultrasound results showed indeed that the baby was breech, which means her feet were facing down instead of her head—not the safest way for a baby to be born. Also, she was showing signs of stress. With each contraction, her heart rate was slowing to an alarming rate.

She said that the baby needed to be delivered now, and that it was my option how to deliver since I was fully dilated. I could attempt to deliver the baby naturally, which would only pose about a ten percent risk to the baby of something going wrong, or I could deliver by C-section, which posed a ten percent chance of something happening to me. Of course, being a mother, I chose to risk myself. I didn't want any chance of my baby being harmed in any way. As the medical team left to get prepped for the emergency surgery, I immediately started to cry; I hadn't anticipated a C-section at ALL and was afraid. I had never had surgery of any kind up until now. Would I be put to sleep? Would I wake up? Would I have a horrible scar for life? I woke up Gerald and told him the news; he was also worried and not sure what to expect.

Karen calmly took us both by the hands and prayed with us, telling us that God was in charge and that he would protect us and this baby. We relaxed as she encouraged and hugged us. I told her I wanted her there with me as well. She and Gerald got fully suited up in gowns, shoes, and little hats. They both looked so cute.

As doctors administered my epidural, and wheeled me into the delivery room, I realized I would be awake and talking thorough the whole process! I thought that was strange. They put a curtain up in front of my belly and Gerald positioned himself over on the other side so he could watch everything. Karen took my hand and continued to pray. I was so grateful to have her there. It amazed me that she was there for me like she was, more like a mother than even a friend. When I had no mother there to hold my hand, God put Karen in her place, and she whispered that things would be alright and encouraged me, calming my fears. The doctor started cutting and asked me if I could feel anything, which I couldn't. They proceeded to finish the incision and open me up. Gerald's eyes got wide and said that my insides looked like "ground beef." I could feel them reaching around inside of my body, and I felt a "tugging" sensation that was almost painful. They pulled a few times, and then Gerald said he saw her.

"She has so much dark hair!" he exclaimed, which surprised me, because little Gerald had none at birth, save a few blond wisps of hair.

"Wow," I said.

"She's out!" he said.

I didn't hear a cry for what seemed like an eternity. "Is she okay?" I asked, and neither Gerald nor Karen answered. They were just looking, which made me nervous.

"Is she okay?" I asked again, starting to get nervous.

Then I heard it...a high pitched mewling, like a little kitten.

"Yes," they finally said.

"Praise God!" Karen said, laughing and hugging Gerald.

Gerald said later that her cord was wrapped around her neck twice and she was completely gray when she was born. She looked dead. After they removed the cord and she could breathe, her color quickly changed to pale, almost white. They brought her over to me, and her face looked straight at my face ... She had such a perfect round little head (a result of the C-section) and wide eyes that were already looking all around. She was perfect. I fell in love at first sight.

They gave us the stats: Born at 6:37 a.m. on August 23, 1992, she weighed in at six pounds, thirteen ounces, and twenty inches long. A cute little petite thing, but still perfectly normal in height and weight. To this day, I think the reason they measured her small is because they didn't realize she was breech. I was also so glad I didn't choose to have her naturally, because with the cord wrapped around her neck and her in distress, she may not have made it. From the beginning, I thought, she must be really special for the devil to have tried to prevent her from even coming into this world!

I couldn't stop staring at her—she was so beautiful. She had big, dark, almost black observant eyes and with her pale skin she looked like Betty Boop. She was also so calm and barely cried at all. She just stared at everything. Her hair was so long and dark, that you could not see her scalp. I could put it in barrettes, which was also unexpected. I thought about little G and now my new baby girl, and I marveled at how two children could look and act so different who came from the same two parents! I couldn't believe she was actually here. From the beginning, all the odds had been against her: I wasn't supposed to go back to Georgia and get pregnant. I wasn't supposed to have another baby at eighteen. I wasn't supposed to have a healthy delivery. And yet, God had the last say. Here she was—lovely, healthy, and whole—and I prayed over her right then that her life would be one of peace, love, and happiness. I also bound up the enemy in her life, who so obviously wanted her gone. For what reason, I didn't know, but it was apparent to me that she would one day do great things! Tears came to my eyes when I thought about the fact that I almost got rid of her.

I still hadn't chosen a name but was pretty sure I liked Briana best. Gerald and I were still debating even in the delivery room. However, after Karen went home and got David, they appeared in my hospital room with flowers and balloons later that morning. One of the balloons had the words "Happy Birthday, Ashley" on them. Gerald and I just looked at each other and smiled.

It was decided…Ashley Nicole Williams it was!!!

CHAPTER 11

Homecoming

WHEN WE BECOME PARENTS, suddenly we are flooded with an extremely overwhelming sense of love and sacrifice for another human being that we may never have known we possessed! It starts to create in us the urge to do and be better, and gives us motivation to succeed. For my two small children, I wanted to be a "SuperWoman" who could be and do everything. I felt that they deserved all the time, love, and attention I didn't receive myself, and I was determined to give it to them. I also wanted to raise them up to know and love the Lord, something no one in our family had done before this. It would be a new thing for this generation: to have married parents who are putting God first, and raising up their children as Christians. I was foraging paths that had never even been attempted in my lineage; the prospect thrilled and excited me! It's still only a fraction of the love that God has for us. He feels all of these things for us, his children, and more. He wants us to do great things, love him, and be protected and secure our entire lives. He longs to see us blessed—we have only to walk in obedience. When unexpected things happen, we still can trust him and know he will work it out for good!

There was a verse I had memorized during this time from listening to it repetitively on the kids' praise tapes: "*And we know that in all things*

God works for the good of those who love him, who have been called according to his purpose"(Romans 8:28). It was just up to me to believe it.

Soon after giving birth, I became ill with an infection from the C-section and spent the next week in the hospital with a one-hundred-and-one-plus temperature. I was in such pain that I couldn't even cough lightly. I had a couple of visitors, but mostly I was on my own. I didn't even see Gerald for the rest of the week. Apparently, he was busy with school, and it was his birthday week, which I wasn't able to spend with him, which saddened me. The nurses were also extremely rude. They never came in once to check on the baby, and wouldn't even wheel her next to me when they left the room. They often left her way across the entire room, requiring me to get up and slowly walk to her whenever she cried. Anyone who has had a C-section knows that when you try to walk soon after, it feels as if your insides are falling out—very hard for about a week or two. If I called the nurses for anything, they responded harshly or never came, and I was so ill and tired that I didn't know what to do. One nurse came in, and when I asked her for juice, proceeded to put her hands on her hips and inform me, "We are not your slaves." This was already such an overwhelming time for me, I broke down in tears, praying to God to help me.

My mother and father both called to see how I was, and when I told them what was going on, they were outraged. They both called the hospital yelling and cursing, threatening to sue. Immediately the nurses' attitudes changed, and I had no further problems. Apparently they simply saw me as another teen mom with no support, which in my opinion is no excuse for such mistreatment. Regardless of how they tried to make it "right" after that, I vowed to never use nor recommend this hospital to anyone again.

I still had a wedding to plan in less than two weeks. Most of my plans for the wedding were made by calling around in the phone book. With our financial situation, there really wasn't much we could afford, so I found a little chapel in Corona, the city where Gerald lived, that was approximately $150 for four hours of use. It would be a rose garden ceremony with pastor included. The catch was that only fifteen people would be allowed to come to the actual ceremony. Because I didn't have much access to the outside world, I left it up to Gerald to invite the people. I invited four: my parents and Karen and David. Everyone else would be welcome to come to the reception, which would be in a rented space in a shopping center. My mom's friend June was making an income doing professional party planning, and both women offered to decorate.

One day while I was still in the hospital, Gerald's mother called me about my wedding, telling me that Gerald's older sister had just gotten engaged and was also getting married on that same date, and asked me to change my wedding date. I was really upset, and slightly offended, especially this close to my wedding date, but I respectfully told her no, that we had decided on that day many weeks before, and that all of the reservations had already been made.

Gerald's sister decided to move her wedding to that Sunday, but I noticed the attitude that I was inconveniencing them by even having our wedding. None of his family acted as if our wedding was anything to be celebrated at all. The fact that we were so young may have partly been to blame for why they behaved that way, but I kept hearing rumors that his mother said I had "trapped" Gerald because of his dreams of becoming a basketball player. And, according to them, my parenting skills were substandard, I had a bad attitude, and I was too possessive and controlling of Gerald. (*In other words, I didn't want him hanging out, going to clubs, and seeing other women.)* I tried to overlook these things and continue to be respectful, but to hear gossip like Gerald "only wants to marry her for the children" sometimes angered me, deeply wounded me, and made me want to have nothing to do with them. However, for the sake of Gerald as well as the children, I held my tongue. I hadn't been raised in a large family, and I hoped that maybe once we got married and they saw that I was a Christian now, that this would possibly bring our families closer—especially since they claimed to be Christians as well.

I always felt that instead of judging and criticizing me, his mother and older sister should have helped and mentored me in all areas in which I wasn't equipped, especially since I was just fifteen years old when they met me, and I couldn't possibly know much about being a wife and mother. Thank God that Karen came into my life to encourage me and support me in learning so many important things! Contrary to popular opinion, maintaining a home and being a wife and a mother are not *inborn* abilities. These things do not come "naturally" in young women, especially someone like me who did not see it modeled properly. Someone had to come along and patiently guide, nurture, and train me up in these things, and it consistently hurt my feelings to always hear that I wasn't the greatest housekeeper or mother at age eighteen, especially when I tried so hard. I vowed that regardless of what anyone thought, my kids would be my focus and I would overcome all of my obstacles, and be a good wife and mother, regardless of who else believed in me. I had God, and that was all that mattered.

After my fever went down under a hundred, they finally released me from the hospital—just one week until the wedding! I was happy to get to go home, settle the baby in, and begin my search for a wedding dress. I knew I would need a larger size because I hadn't lost my baby weight, but I wanted to find something that wouldn't make me look huge. Karen and David came to pick me up and, once home, I settled the baby into her little crib. She looked so tiny and adorable, and was such a good and peaceful baby who rarely cried. I had one-on-one time to spend with her because Gerald had taken little G the day I was in labor to his family's house to stay with them. He still lived with his mother. I missed my son terribly, but knew they were good with children and would take good care of him. He came to visit and brought little Gerald with him. He was dressed in a sweat suit, too hot for August, and his hair was uncombed. I changed him, brushed his hair, and let him see the baby. He kissed her—it was so sweet.

Taking care of this baby was pretty easy. She slept a lot, and when awake was calm and alert. I had my CD player, and would play my Crystal Lewis all day long. At night, it was playing also next to her crib. Funny, the only time she cried was when the cassette came to the end and the music stopped. If I got up and flipped over the tape, she would go right back to sleep; I was amazed by that. She seemed to love Christian music herself!

Karen and David seemed to really love her, and Karen had a little surprise for me of her own: She was pregnant again too! I was happy for her. "God should bless you with lots of children because you are such good parents," I told her. With her own girls, she was already so extremely patient and kind.

"I feel the same way about you," she said, which touched me. No one had every called me a good mother before; it made me happy that she noticed. I felt so blessed to have them in my life.

~~~~~~~

> *"He fulfills the desires of those who fear him; he hears their cry and saves them"*
> (Psalm 145:19).

I remember so many times when I was younger that my dad said he would come and pick me up, but didn't show up. I would wait for hours on end, lonely and upset. It happened that way too with my stepmother. She promised many times to bring my younger brother and sister to see me, and they never came. I would stare out the windows for hours, and call their phones repeatedly, with no response. The tears I cried, and the neglect and anger I felt were intense, even as a child. But there were also times when my dad would surprise me, and pop up out of nowhere. These were my favorite times, because they were unexpected. I would light up like a Christmas tree, and excitedly brag to my friends that my dad was *here!* Sometimes we wait on God that way, and sometimes God doesn't seem to show up the times we want Him to, and we feel abandoned and neglected—but other times He shows up out of nowhere, and causes us much happiness and surprise blessings, many times even when we are least deserving. God longs to bless us just as any earthly father should. He wants to see us happy and content, and shower us with love and blessings. But many of us are living in spiritual rebellion, and not making an effort to love Him, or let Him lead. With obedience comes healing, and wholeness. God will hear your pain and suffering if you cry out to Him and, like a protective parent, will come to your defense and help you through. It's just a matter of *trusting* and *fearing* Him.

So that weekend, Karen and I decided to go on the search for wedding dresses. This was much harder than I expected. Because I was still healing, I tired quickly and couldn't stay on my feet for too long. Also, I was in a size ten!—which for me was big, considering I had previously worn a three. I couldn't find anything that didn't make my stomach look huge. Finally, my budget was minimal: I had $350 for everything. My mother was helping pay some expenses as well as helping decorate the reception hall. I was grateful for that because it would help save money. Most of the dresses I liked wouldn't fit right, looked funny on me, or cost too much. We went to four different stores before I became discouraged. One dress I found was off-white with lacey material, and I put it on hold, but I wasn't really excited about it.

Seeing that I was discouraged, Karen began to pray with, and for me. She prayed right there in the car for God to help me, and show Himself, and that I would find the perfect dress. After praying, she hesitantly asked: "Don't be mad at me for asking, but would you consider looking at a few thrift stores? Sometimes they have really great deals."

Karen had always been a great steward of her money. She had a monthly allowance, and often took us all to thrift stores where I found great items for lil Gerald. Costa Mesa was a rather wealthy area anyway; their thrift stores were always filled with "high end" articles and Karen always found the best deals. At that point, I was desperate and open to anything.

"Yeah, okay, sure. Nothing wrong with that. Let's try it!" I said, relieved to have a suggestion.

We went to a small thrift store that she knew of. It seemed to have a fair selection of party dresses, and even a couple of cute wedding dresses. Karen started talking to the lady behind the counter, asking her about her selections as I was about to try on three dresses I found.

"Hold on!" the lady said. "I have one dress in the storage room that you may like."

I waited, and she came back with a huge Jessica McClintock designer dress bag.

"This is my first day back to work after being gone for a month. If you hadn't come today when I was here, you may not have known about it. Only I did." As she unzipped it, we all gasped. It was pure white, off the shoulder, silky, and tight around the middle with a full bodice and long train! I couldn't believe that it was in a thrift store. It was better than anything I had tried on that day. I grabbed the dress excitedly, and Karen and I rushed to the dressing room.

"Pray that it fits!" I cried. We both started praying as I stepped into the dress. As we pulled it up, it was so comfortable, and the material felt great. It was so big and pretty, it looked like a princess gown.

"Okay...let's try to zip it!!" said Karen, calling on the Lord again.

It zipped perfectly.

We squealed and hugged in delight. The dress suddenly made me look as if I had never given birth! It cinched my waist in such a way that it gave the illusion of a trim figure, and it had a huge pretty bow in the back. As I stepped out of the dressing room, everyone gasped.

"That dress looks like it was MADE for you!" the manager exclaimed.

I felt so beautiful. It was perfect. I didn't want to take it off!

Now the big question remained. "How much is it?" I asked, again saying a silent prayer.

"For you, because it's so perfect for you, I will give it to you for…$150."

I almost fainted. This big, beautiful fairytale Jessica McClintock dress complete with train and garment bag—for only $150?

I jumped for joy. Indeed God was already blessing my steps and giving me favor.

It just so happened that only that particular lady, that particular day knew about that dress in the storage room, and it fit me perfectly. It reminded me of the story of Esther, whom God gave favor to, and put her in the position of being pampered and treated like a queen, despite her humble beginnings. Right now, I felt like a pampered princess. God seemed to be smiling down on me, and for the first time in my life, I felt that God was gifting me for my faith and determination to do right in my life.

Although initially I was unsure about whether I should marry Gerald, I suddenly felt a peace in my spirit that God would make things alright in the end. He was apparently confirming in my spirit that this union was something that He would bless. Everything in planning my wedding seemed to be easy and move quickly from that day forward.

When anxiety was great within me, your consolation brought joy to my soul.
~Psalm 94:19

CHAPTER 12

Wedding Bells

THE NEXT COUPLE OF WEEKS went by like a whirlwind in my memory. Possibly because I was so busy with last minute planning and taking care of a new baby. I was both exhausted and excited. I just wanted everything to be perfect on the limited budget that I had.

A couple of days before the wedding, my mother flew out from Georgia and brought her best friend June over to visit. They were excited to see the baby and were finally able to meet Karen and David. Neither of my parents was sure why I was living with this family, because I had never been open in discussing it, but Mom was really cordial, and nice to them, much to my relief.

During the week before the wedding, Gerald's sister apparently broke up with her fiancé and called off her wedding. Prior to this, I was over Gerald's house and noticed that his entire family from Memphis had come to town for the wedding, and I actually watched them wrap gifts and discuss preparations. Strangely, I also noticed that not one person acknowledged our own wedding that was to take place that weekend.

When I brought up that we were getting married too, Gerald's mom hesitantly asked me if I needed her to do anything. I told her I would love it if she could bring the cake, and that she and her sisters could cook something for the guests. She agreed, so I felt relieved that that was one less thing I would have to worry about. It was hard planning a wedding on my own, but I was looking forward to having our families meet and get to know each other.

After Gerald's sister cancelled her wedding, though, the family just stayed in town to attend ours. I really don't think this was a planned thing…seeing that none of those beautifully wrapped gifts ended up at our wedding.

The night before our wedding, I set an appointment with a friend of mine who was a hairdresser. She was going to come to the house and do my hair, which I was happy about. I also scheduled a manicure and pedicure, and Karen's friend was coming over to do my makeup. Everything was set. We went to David's Bridal where I picked out the flowers, a cute decoration for my hair, and my jewelry. We picked out a deejay through a friend, and Karen asked about what I planned to do regarding drinking at the reception.

I had forgotten about that. I grew up seeing those things regularly and wasn't sure how to handle it. I didn't want to offend Karen and David by having people drinking there, because I held their feelings in such high regard. I asked her what she thought I should do. She suggested apple cider, so my mother planned to order cartons of that for the guests and toasts. I wasn't old enough to legally drink anyway, so it didn't bother me much.

My mom and June set out to decorate the store-front shopping center that we would have use of for exactly four hours. She also rented a limo to pick us up, and take us to both the wedding and reception. Gerald and I made our plans to take a trip to Vegas for our honeymoon, which was funny because I wasn't old enough to gamble. Funny how I was old enough to marry and raise a family, but not old enough to do much else!

One of the things Gerald and I really hadn't taken time to discuss was where we would live. I knew that once I got married I wasn't going to be staying with Karen and David any longer, but Gerald was in school and playing ball full time. We decided that until we got on our feet, we would stay with Gerald's family. They had a comfortable room in the back of the house that they had converted from a garage into a family den. We would save money and eventually get an apartment. Gerald's mom had six kids who all lived in the home, and her oldest daughter had two children as well at that time, pregnant with a third. So there would be eleven of us there. I just hoped that Gerald would work hard to get us our own place. I was getting financial assistance from the government that totaled a little over $800 per month, and medical care was free for the children. Gerald also worked with an attorney and a doctor on insurance cases (bringing them clients), and earned a commission that sometimes brought in $1,500 in one month. This was a lot of money for us, and we had very few bills and expenses, so money wasn't an issue for us initially.

The day of our wedding, September 5, 1992, turned out to be beautiful. My mother was taking over helping with the baby while I got ready. My hair had grown a lot from pregnancy and being worn in a ponytail so it was healthy and thick, and so pretty when she did it. The makeup artist was also very skilled. I didn't wear makeup at the time and was afraid it wouldn't look natural, but she did a great job with light pinks and salmons that made me look really natural and pretty—I loved it! The wedding was scheduled at 2 p.m. and we had only four hours to rent the place out or be charged extra fees, so time was of the essence. I called Gerald early that morning with all of the info, and he assured me he would be there.

As if getting married under these conditions wasn't stressful enough, several things happened that day that further increased my stress level, and required prayer. The first thing: Gerald's mom called and asked me if I *"really* still needed" her to get a cake and cook the meal for the wedding. She said she didn't think she could find a cake at the last minute, and hadn't really thought of what to make. I was surprised, to say the least. This was the day of my wedding, and I had told her about it weeks before, giving her plenty of time. I told her yes, I depended on her to do what she agreed to, and that I couldn't handle any changes right now because I had no alternative options, and also that I was getting ready for my wedding in a few hours.

She sighed as if put out by my request, and said she would try.
My mother, tired from staying up all night decorating my reception hall, replied upon hearing that, "That's all she has to do, and she can't do that?" I just told her it was now handled, and to ignore it. My mom was very "no nonsense." She didn't mind a confrontation, yet also was extremely professional, and to the point. My mother shook her head. She was already annoyed that the family had never bought my children gifts of any kind, nor participated in any way helping with the wedding costs. She tried to keep her feelings to herself, but I could tell already that there was tension brewing between the two mothers.

My mother and her friend June agreed to keep little Gerald and Ashley while we went on the honeymoon. I gave her detailed written instructions on their schedules, yet I was still nervous about leaving my new baby overnight at just two weeks old. They were very good with babies though, and assured me that all would be well under control and encouraged me to enjoy myself. As I put on my dress, they told me how beautiful I looked.

I wanted to be an hour early to the ceremony, and see everything. The limo came to pick me up, and I took one last long look around my room that had been my home for almost six months. My Bible rested on my little desk, and I remembered when I first walked into the room, and was so resistant to the changes that were going on in my life. Now I was filled with sudden sadness that I would never sleep in this room again.

Karen and David hugged and complimented me, and said they would meet us there. Looking back now, I didn't get to say much to them in the last week or so before the wedding—everything was so hurried and rushed. However, I could see a hint of both pride and sadness in their eyes, and it touched me deeply.

As I walked out to the waiting limo, I felt beautiful in my big princess dress—so different from the pregnant girl I had been the last year. I smiled and waved to everyone, got in, and said a prayer in the limo. I felt that God was with me, and that He would let everything work out just fine.

We arrived at the church at 1 p.m. and the garden was beautiful. They had set up for fifteen seats, and there was a pretty gazebo. They had me fill out the marriage certificate and explained the whole process. I called Gerald several times with no answer.

At 1:45 p.m.—just fifteen minutes before the ceremony was to start—people began arriving and being seated. Gerald finally answered my pages and calls. He told me he was at the mall getting his suit!

I was upset. He didn't do that until now? He said he would be there in thirty minutes. I told him that it was supposed to start in fifteen minutes, and he asked me to stall. The problem was that this place charged for lateness, and they set the time back for the reception hall rental. He apologized and said he would be there quickly.

He arrived two hours late.

Although I was really angry and considered calling the wedding off, I simply tried to shrug it off. My dad was there to walk me down the aisle, and the ceremony went off without a hitch.

Once the music started and I walked down the aisle, my mind calmed … I looked over and saw Karen and David looking at me with love, and tears in their eyes. My mind reflected on the love and encouragement they had showed me over the past six months, and it amazed me that these people could become so important to me, in such a short time. I felt sadness that I would no longer be in their house and a part of their little family unit, but at the same time excited that I would now be moving forward to starting one of my own.

At the end of the aisle, Gerald looked at me as though I was the most beautiful person he had ever seen. He didn't take his eyes off of me as he said his vows, and I could see that he loved me, deeply. We were both very young and still possibly didn't know what real love and commitment entailed yet, but our hopes were to have a future that could serve as a model to our children. I felt good that things would be done right in God's eyes. As I looked into Gerald's eyes, all of the pressure and stress melted away, and I was just happy to be there with him, vowing my life to stand by his side.

My parents cried, Gerald's mom sang, and everyone relaxed, and enjoyed the beautiful day. As I watched everyone smiling and talking and taking photos, I fought back the tears. My dad came over to hug me, and I could see his eyes were rimmed in red.

"I'm not a Riggins anymore!" I exclaimed to him.

He started to cry, and we hugged tightly.

What started off as stressful and chaotic, God turned into a time of joy and celebration. It wasn't huge, elaborate, or expensive, and may not have been the wedding of my dreams, but right then, in my eyes…everything was perfect.

CHAPTER 13

Goodbyes

...Do not fear, for I have redeemed you; I have summoned you by name; you are mine. When you pass through the waters, I will be with you; and when you pass through the rivers, they will not sweep over you. When you walk through the fire, you will not be burned; the flames will not set you ablaze. For I am the Lord your God, the Holy One of Israel, your Savior... ~Isaiah 43:1-3

SETTING UP MY ABORTION APPOINTMENT six months earlier, I never would have guessed in a million years that my life would end up the way it did. I never thought I would not only have a beautiful new baby girl, but a husband, be a Christian, and be given a whole new loving family that would strengthen and heal my old wounds and insecurities. Life is all about choices, and when I decided on the path to keeping my daughter, the rewards were overwhelming. I felt that God was pleased with my obedience, and although I wasn't naïve enough to believe that we would just "ride off into the sunset" and have no problems in the future, I knew we were beginning to lay a more solid and stable foundation for future generations after us. My own parents hadn't been married. Gerald's parents hadn't been married. We hadn't seen our grandparents married. There were no real guidelines that we knew to follow, so we decided we wanted to create our own path.

In the limo ride to the reception, we were happy and excited, and Gerald told me I was beautiful. We felt like it was such a new beginning for us, and we were ready to take it on together. We knew there were many who were against the marriage and said that we were too young and had no hope of making it, but we decided to look beyond that and try to figure out what God had to say about it. From what we were seeing, God was blessing our union and had given us the gifts of Karen and David to model for us what it meant to be a husband and wife team who lovingly submitted to God and each other. Although initially Gerald was not yet saved, he respected the example that was set and the hopes I had for training our children up in God. Somehow we both knew that the decisions we made from now on would have an impact for generations to come, and neither of us wanted to mess that up.

The reception was beautifully decorated with our chosen colors: teal, black, and white, and my mother and June had even formed a huge balloon arch over the reception table. I was thrilled at how great of a job they had done…it looked great! Many members of my family I hadn't seen in years showed up to celebrate.

Gerald's mother showed up two hours late to the reception. Although I was expecting her to cook, she brought a tray of "pigs in a blanket" hot dogs, obviously thrown together last minute. She also brought a cake from Kroger, which had my name spelled wrong on it. Add all that to the fact that none of the family brought gifts. I was rather disappointed in the lack of effort put in. When my mother asked her why her family had not brought one gift, her response to my mother was, "Because…her gift is *marrying my son.*"

This began years of tension between our families.

Starting that day, it was obvious to me that many people around us didn't want us married. When Gerald came back, people were actually asking him right there at the wedding why he married me, and telling him he was too young, and that it was a mistake. My mother was furious that his family was making these sorts of comments, and grabbing whole bottles of sparkling cider and walking out with them, and no one was dancing. The atmosphere was not one of love and compassion but of judgment and negativity, and it saddened me, after I had just experienced such a positive experience. The pain was building up in me almost to the point of tears, as I was suddenly overwhelmed with the obvious lack of support for our union. How could we have a happy marriage without the support of those around us?

I decided to put my mind on positive things—and the best part of the reception was the fact that Gerald had brought little G to the wedding. I hadn't seen him since giving birth, and I had missed him. He missed me too, because he screamed and cried whenever they took him out of my arms. Much of the reception, I held him. I even danced with him on the dance floor. Soon, I began to get tired, since I had recently given birth. By the time we left for Vegas, I had dark circles under my eyes, and my exhaustion was evident.

I didn't know what to make of the reception, and my mother decided she would have another the next month that she would plan, and invite all of our family members. Her guests gave me over $300 in cash, and gifts, and for that, I was grateful. My mother ended up paying for the additional time on the rental hall as well as the deejay. She felt as if Gerald's family should have offered to pay for something, but we knew that was out of the question. It was obvious that this marriage was not something they supported.

The enemy always seeks to have you immediately second-guess your decisions. In the Bible it says he is like the scavenger birds that seek to "pluck" up the biblical words and lessons that have not been sown deeply into your heart (Matthew 13:4). The wedding reception, and all of the subtle animosity that I had been shown, really made me unsure that this marriage is what God had for me.

But I tried to overlook it and focus on what God had done, and was doing for me. It became a matter of having faith in the things I could not see, and looking past the things that were on the surface. As long as God blessed our union, I couldn't worry about who else didn't.

As the wedding drew to a close and I prepared to leave the wedding and get in the limo to head to Vegas, I kissed my babies goodnight and I hugged Karen and David again, thanking them for all they had done for me. There was so much more that I wanted to say, things that words could not express in those brief moments…but time was so busy and overwhelming. I knew I would see them again when I went over to pick up my items, so I left it at that.

It was time to go off into our future as husband and wife.

I was eighteen years old, a wife, mother, and new Christian. I didn't know what the future held, but I now knew WHO held my future, and that confidence gave me a peace that surpassed all understanding.

PART 4

LAYING FOUNDATIONS

I shall be telling this with a sigh
Somewhere ages and ages hence:
Two roads diverged in a wood, and I,
I took the one less traveled by,
…And that has made all the difference.

CHAPTER 14

The Newlywed Life

EVERY CHOICE WE MAKE takes us down a path that will shape our character and eventually determine our destiny. Within six short months, I had taken a path from rebellious child to responsible woman, and it was all due to the decisions I had made when faced with my own personal "fork in the road." We all have them—the option to choose between two paths that may not have clear directives. Life is summed up by a series of these choices and decisions that we make every day. Each choice will either take us closer to the destiny God has for us or farther away from it.

We don't always have to take the paths that "Momma and them" took before us. In Christian settings, you might hear that something is a "generational curse"—that the reason you're a certain way is because others in your family were that way and have been for many generations, and so it's destined for you and yours to go that way, too. For example, if your father and grandfather were alcoholics, then it's written in stone that you will be too. While such generational curses do exist, and breaking free of them can be very difficult indeed, you need to remember that you always have a choice, and that it is not destiny for you to follow in the same cursed footsteps as those before you.

One thing that is important to remember is that Christ bore all curses on the cross—even generational ones. Yet it is hard for us to believe and claim, and we continue to act as if we are helplessly destined to repeat certain bad habits, and behaviors. But His word says that He took all curses upon Himself at the cross. They are no longer ours to bear!

"...having canceled the written code, with its regulations, that was against us and that stood opposed to us; he took it away, nailing it to the cross" (Colossians 2:14).

My father was a pimp, drug dealer, and womanizer, who eventually used drugs. If I had believed the talk that you will always be a product of your parents and your environment, I would have stayed where I was, and just caved in to that life. I was raised in a long line of single, dysfunctional mothers as well—I could easily have resigned myself to the fact that that's just "how we are" and let violence, and promiscuity have its way in my life because that's what I had grown up seeing.

Gerald's father did not meet him till he was twenty-four years old, and many people told him when he was a child that he would end up "dead or in jail." Generational curses or verbal curses spoken over you need to be confronted—and broken. Instead of giving in to the curses spoken over your life and the belief that you have no choice but to become just like your parents, you can actually decide to take your life in a completely different direction—to stop the tide and redirect it. I made a conscious decision to forge a different path, like the character in the Robert Frost poem. The bitter roots of dysfunction ran deep in my family tree, but one thing I learned about trees is that if you cut one off at the root, it doesn't necessarily have to die; it can actually be regrown if you put it in water for several months and wait it out. In our own lives, it is possible to cut off the dead, diseased and decayed roots of our past and toss it out so that we can get rid of those things that negatively affect the next generation.

Even Jesus mentioned the importance of removing those things and people that do not contribute to his purpose:

> *He cuts off every branch in me that bears no fruit, while every branch that does bear fruit he prunes so that it will be even more fruitful. You are already clean because of the word I have spoken to you. Remain in me, as I also remain in you. No branch can bear fruit by itself; it must remain in the vine. Neither can you bear fruit unless you remain in me.* ~John 15: 2-4

It's not easy, either. Once you make a decision to believe God's word, the enemy quickly attacks and tries to plant doubt. For several months after our wedding, I lived with Gerald's family, and they were not kind, or loving to me whatsoever. Gerald was in school all day toward evening, so I was stranded there a lot as he took my car with him. The family refused to take me anywhere; I had to catch buses and walk when my children had appointments or call Gerald out of school. Once, I couldn't get a ride in the rain, so I called the police to take us home because I didn't want to walk in the rain with a toddler.

The family refused to let me eat the food, even posting signs on the fridge saying, "Don't eat our food." They vandalized our wedding cake that I had kept in the freezer for our one year anniversary. I lost twenty pounds in a few short months. They talked about me in rooms nearby so that I could hear, and told the younger children (Gerald's young siblings) that my room was still the den, and that they could come in and out any time because it's not my house and I don't 'pay rent'. They encouraged the children to say that to me if I protested the early morning noise right next to the couch bed I slept in. I constantly heard,

"If you don't like it, get out!" yelled throughout the house, obviously directed at me. Needless to say, it was a totally different environment, a stark contrast to the loving, accepting Christian household I had just come from. I was treated better by strangers, than those who were now family.

I had no idea what to do, so I tried to stay in the den in my little corner with my two babies. They complained about my son being hyper, said he had ADD and needed counseling. I was constantly accused of not cleaning the house (that I wasn't even considered living in). I cleaned up after myself and my kids, and kept all of my things in one corner, away from view of anyone coming and going. They made it clear that I had no room, nor any privacy, and the den I slept in would be open to anyone as early or as late as they chose to stay in there. They would complain to Gerald about my lack of help around the house, and I promptly told Gerald that I wasn't cleaning a home I wasn't even allowed to sleep comfortably in, or doing dishes I couldn't eat on. I was nice, and young, but I wasn't going to allow myself to be treated unkindly either. Gerald hesitated to get involved, and instead chose to stay gone until late into the evening. One time I heard Gerald's sister tell his uncle that she *hated* me. I did not understand this, since I never disrespected them or talked rudely to them or their children. My heart ached. I felt as if I was spiraling into a depression after a short time. I missed the love, laughter, and peaceful spirit of Karen and David's home, and the way in which they loved and embraced me. I couldn't even discuss this with my parents, because I didn't want an all-out war, and didn't believe in telling your family about your marital issues, so I just kept it inside, and often cried to myself when I was alone.

I really tried to overlook the treatment I was receiving, because the Spirit I had lived with in Karen and David's home taught me about forgiveness and peace, but it really was hard. I was not used to this kind of treatment. I did continue to hold my tongue, though, and be respectful. I would buy Gerald's little brothers and sisters Christian tapes and videos, but I was laughed at and talked about for trying to be "holy." They said I went to a Catholic church and refused to visit. I was confused because these were also people who said they were Christian, and when I was saved, I assumed that all Christians just automatically loved and helped each other the way Karen and David modeled to me.

I prayed continually that God would help me, and after two months, God heard my cries. I was eating out one day with some friends of ours from high school—Shelia, my buddy, and her husband Julian, Gerald's best friend. We had all met in high school and were a foursome. Julian and Sheila fell in love and got married. I was having lunch with them alone, and they asked me how things were going. I couldn't hold it in any longer and burst into tears right there at the lunch table. I was crying about what was going on at Gerald's mom's house, and also out of frustration because I had no one else to talk to. My friend Sheila immediately went into action. She called the manager at the complex in Fontana where they lived and asked her to help me. I got the keys for less than $300 move-in. And my move-in date just so happened to fall on my nineteenth birthday. I felt like those keys were a birthday gift from God straight to me! On top of that, Julian and Sheila lived there with their young babies, so we got to be neighbors as well! I was so grateful. It was a one bedroom apartment, very simple, but it was ours. Initially we had no furniture, but I sat on the floor—and was happy to do it. Within a week, Sheila's family had donated to us a house full of furniture, along with some things we picked up at a thrift store. I could finally breathe, and felt as if my life was now beginning. We were all set!

CHAPTER 15

A Call to Leave

KAREN AND DAVID CALLED me shortly before I moved into my own apartment and told me they were moving to Idaho. They said they were leaving to help a pastor of theirs set up a church down there, and they would be leaving ASAP. It's the type of thing you would expect them to do, as committed and loyal as they were, but it devastated me. In my mind, I wasn't strong enough to have them go so far across the country. Right now, I could pick up and visit when things were stressful or call them for advice, but Idaho was states away and I didn't know what to do. I was beyond hurt, and although I appreciated that they felt God was calling them in another direction, I really didn't want to see them leave California.

They came over before they left town, to say goodbye.

I don't remember much about this meeting, because honestly I blocked a lot of it out. It was too painful, and I never liked to think of it again. I do remember them coming over to Gerald's mom's house and I met them outside. For some reason, I didn't want them to go in there, because I felt they were too sweet to even go into that environment. We stood in the driveway and they gave me a card, and I think I wrote them a letter.

As we hugged in the driveway, I couldn't hold back the tears. I felt like my beloved parents were leaving me behind. I was filled with dread and fear about what my future held. These people had been my support, my friends, my parents, my encouragers, and my mentors for half a year. I couldn't image my life without them in it. I told them I wanted them to be Ashley's godparents, and they asked me what that means. I said that it means they will teach my child about God and be a religious role model and example, and they said, "Okay, but that's your job. You be the example, and you continue to teach your child about God all her life." That's a great lesson I learned. As parents, we are honored with caring for these wonderful beings and are not to pass the responsibility off to anyone else. We are their stewards, assigned to train them up in the Lord (Proverbs 22:6), and it was my job to be mother, teacher, pastor, and all those other roles; I couldn't expect anyone else to do it for me.

Gerald and I had both been left to fend for ourselves by mothers who seemed to put self before us and our needs, and we vowed never to do those things to our own children. We wanted to be there every step of the way: leading, guiding, and teaching different lessons for the next generation.

Things were coming to a close. I was getting my own place, Karen and David were leaving, and I didn't know what lay ahead for my little family. Karen took me aside and assured me I would be okay. She told me they loved me, and she told me that God had a plan for me, and that she never met another teen like me … I was special. She said I would be a great wife and mother, and that I just needed to keep God first.

As we hugged, my mind flooded with all of our cherished moments ... the stick-shift driving lessons up and down the hills of Costa Mesa as we screamed and laughed wildly and I barely made it up the hills and sped around corners ... the nights she stayed up to talk with me into the wee hours about God's love and forgiveness ... our talks of our past as we fed our children together ... our shared joy as we roasted marshmallows ... as she proudly took pictures after my baptism ... the times she taught me to bake bread and cook delicious meals ... our daily outings as we toted the kids down the street in the red wagon and laughed as they held on tight to each other, looking wide-eyed with excitement ... the emotional grip when she held my hand as I delivered my daughter, and again as she prayed over my finding the "perfect" wedding dress ... and the look in her eyes as she lovingly watched me walk down the aisle to meet my husband.

What could they do more than they had done for me? They literally showed me love, guidance, patience, encouragement, and wisdom at every major turning point in my life, and they released me as they should, although just yet I didn't want to release them. They felt confident that I was ready to fly and leave the nest, but I still wasn't quite sure if I had wings yet.

Sometimes God doesn't allow us to depend on anyone outside of Him. Just when we get dependent on something or someone other than Him, He tends to push us out of our comfort zone and keep us moving toward our destiny. I understood now that this was their calling. If I hadn't gotten married when I did, they would have had to leave me anyway. They had many more things to do for the Kingdom. It was all God's perfect timing.

As I watched them climb up into their van and wave to me out of their window, slowly driving off down the street, out of the neighborhood, and out of my life, my heart felt as heavy as a ton of bricks inside my chest and burned so badly I couldn't breathe.

I ran in the house, straight toward the bathroom and closed the door, sat in the dark on the toilet lid, quietly holding my knees and crying until I couldn't cry anymore. The tears fell hot and salty down my face and onto my lap.

Who will keep me on the right path now? I wondered. *Who will love me so unconditionally ever again?* I questioned.

"Who is going to be there for me when I need help, advice, or guidance?" I asked out loud.

The pain in my chest caused my temples to throb and made me feel lightheaded.

In the darkness of the bathroom, I heard a still small voice—it echoed over the sounds of my heartbeat and resonated through my anguish and tears. It slowly pervaded the room, enveloped me in a cloak of comfort, warmth, and understanding. Just two words that I will never forget:

"I AM…"

CHAPTER 16

Full Circle

January 2001

"Myckelle, your client is ready for you now."

I was extremely nervous and unsure of exactly what to say. I had been training for several weeks and practicing the proper procedures and protocol on how to work with each new client, but would quickly learn that everything boils down to intuition and experience, and every case was different.

I went into the small room with my clipboard tightly in hand and sat down with my client. She was a pretty Hispanic girl—young, only seventeen years old, and there because she wanted help. She couldn't see past my professional smile that my insides were a bundle of nerves.

I was a new mentor at the HOPE Pregnancy Resource Center in Woodstock, Georgia. We provided free assistance to women and children who were in crisis situations. A year earlier, we had moved the family from California to Georgia on a word from God that changed our lives. Once we arrived, we started attending a new church, World Changers Church International, and immediately met some amazing people who changed our lives and set some things in motion. One of them, a woman named Darlene, was writing a book and doing workshops called "the Ooh-Ooh Factor." Darlene was unlike anyone I had ever met. The workshops she taught were not only about finding purpose, but so much more—in them she would literally sit down with you, retrace your childhood, and with prayer and prophetic words, show you exactly what your purpose was supposed to be. Most books I'd read on purpose simply told you to look and pray for it, but she actually helped you to *pinpoint* it. It was amazing how during this workshop I realized that my childhood movies, heroes, and even games I played in my alone time all seemed tied into my purpose, which turned out to be changing lives of young girls who were in crisis situations, and who desperately needed to learn how to be mothers and wives—young girls so much like myself at one time.

The first step, Darlene told me, was simply to volunteer in the area of my purpose, and God would do the rest. I found a nice pregnancy clinic in my area and volunteered eight hours per week. Gerald and I had just started a business at home, which opened up our schedules and left our days free. It was perfect timing.

So here I was, taking my very first client after weeks of training and becoming a mentor at the center.

"Hello, I'm Myckelle," I said, smiling, a little relieved to see that she was even more nervous than I was.

I asked all of the required questions, taking down all of her information, finally asking her why she was here today. I assumed it was to get baby items for her young daughter who she brought with her.

"I think I'm pregnant again … and I need a pregnancy test," she said, her eyes filling with tears.

"Sure, okay," I responded. "We provide free pregnancy testing here, and we can do a test today. Let me ask you this: if your test is positive, what are your plans?"

I asked her this question because we helped in providing many needs, such as baby items, counseling, job assistance, medical referrals, adoption referrals, and many other needs, so I wanted to assess what she may need help with.

"I want to get an abortion," she said.

My startled mind was taken back to those fateful words I had uttered years before, when I was not much older than she. I was almost at a loss for words. I stayed calm and took the rest of her information, including the date of her last period, and finally took her to the back bathroom to take the pregnancy test just as I had been trained. My knees were shaking the entire way.

Please don't be pregnant, I silently prayed. I didn't know if I was ready to have this conversation so soon in my new position. It was my first client!

After she completed the test, I brought her back to our little room and showed her the Choices video—the same one I had watched years earlier—as we waited for the results of our own test. While she watched the video, my hands shook as I thought of what she may be thinking in her head. I thought about my own choices, when I was once so afraid and vulnerable, and in my spirit I knew that what I said, or didn't say, in the next thirty minutes could result in the potential loss of life.

I left the room, went to the bathroom, and looked at her test: it was positive.

From all I had learned during training, and looking at her last menstrual cycle, I knew that she was eight weeks along; this baby was fully formed and developed, and had a beating heart and was actively moving. I could practically see it, comfortably nestled in the womb, not knowing that its very life hung in the balance.

I knew that in this young girl's mind, abortion was likely the only option she could imagine, and her youth was working against this baby. I also knew that many times, although we may say we feel helpless and have no other choices, we are just waiting for someone to extend love and help to us. In actuality, deep down inside we just want to be rescued. *"...and call upon me in the day of trouble; I will deliver you, and you will honor Me..."* Psalm 50:15 resounded in my head. God is a deliverer in a time of trouble, and is just waiting on our call.

Lord, this young girl needs you now, I thought. *Help her.*

After the video, I walked back in the room and sat down. I told her that the test was positive.

She broke down in tears. I quickly took her young daughter out of the room into the child care area and asked someone to watch her, and I said a quiet prayer: "Lord, none of me, but all of you. Not my words, but your words through me."

I went back in that room and hugged her as she cried. I held her hand, and listened to her talk of not being able to care for two children, and how she was too young for all this, and didn't know why this was happening to her. She also said she was not going to have another baby, and wanted to do something with her life. She said that this was the worst thing to happen to her right now.

I just listened patiently, until she finally quieted down.

"I understand." I said calmly. "I have been *right where you are!* Almost ten years ago, I was about your age and also expecting my second child, and was angry, scared, and lonely. But let me tell you what God did for me…"

I detailed to her my story of painful choice, and the confusion and guilt I felt at the time. I talked to her about the decision I made to have an abortion, and about my appointment. I also told her my testimony of changing my mind, getting help from a crisis pregnancy center, and about my beautiful daughter's birth. I ended my story with the fact that I was now married with five kids and co-owner of a thriving business. We had a comfortable life, happy children, and had taken in several of our younger family members (and even, ironically, a young Caucasian neighbor boy) and were helping them to learn about and come to Christ. Our children were healthy and well-adjusted. and loved God with all of their hearts.

By the time I finished my story and also told the young girl all that we did there at the center, she looked at me in amazement and wiped her tears. She was silent for a moment, and then she told me that she changed her mind—that she would keep her baby, if we could help her. She allowed me to pray with and for her, and I went out to get her a list of referrals and resources.

"What CAN you do for me?" echoed in my head, as I remembered asking the sweet lady on the other end of the crisis pregnancy line almost ten years earlier. As I closed the door, I let out a deep breath and hurriedly told the other ladies, who jumped up and down and thanked the Lord, which I did too.

What an amazing thing. Everything had truly come full circle!

When that desperate young girl came into the clinic that day, I could see myself in her frightened eyes, but as she spoke I suddenly knew what to say and even how to say it—because I had been there. And it was at that time that I realized my incredible story did not happen to me just for my own benefit, but in order to be a testimony to others. He wanted me to share it and use it to help other young women and girls who needed to hear it!

Approximately two years later, that same young lady walked into the pregnancy center, holding her son. She asked to speak to me.

When I saw her, she hugged and thanked me for my help, understanding, and encouragement. She was so happy. She was holding her young son on her hip and showed him to me. She said if it wasn't for me, her son would not be there. I was blown away. There was an entire person that would grow up and live his life, and she was telling me that if she had not met me that day and I had not said what I said, he would not be here! I was moved to tears… He was a fat, healthy, smiling boy with shiny dark hair and sparkling eyes. I kissed his little round cheeks and told her it was all God, and that all I did was share what He did for me.

I thanked her for being open that day to what God was saying to her through me.

To this day, I will never forget the joy in her eyes as she proudly showed me her baby boy. Yes, maybe she had some trying times and struggled often as we all must do, but in the end, making choices that result in life and not death can never be regretted. She loved her son, just as I loved my daughter, despite the errors we made when we conceived them.

Through my years at the pregnancy center, I experienced many stories like this one of God working through me to help a young woman make a decision to keep her child. Of course, there were also those who still chose to abort. In those cases, as sad as it made me, I would always offer post-abortion counseling, and an ear to listen in case she ever wanted to talk about it or needed help in the future. Many times these young women experienced anger and regret for years after their abortions, sometimes having guilt and nightmares for decades afterward. Counseling tended to help them to be able to talk about their feelings concerning what they had done, and to receive God's mercy and forgiveness, and to work toward forgiving themselves. Abortion is an act that comes with serious long-term implications and scars the soul of a woman—something I had no idea about when I was facing my own decision years earlier.

~~~~~~~

Many of us did not ask to be here, including myself. I was born in 1973, the year that abortion was made legal. Had my mother aborted me, she would have aborted all the potential that came with me. She would have aborted all the lives I changed, all of the people I affected, and the generations that have now come after me. In no way am I condemning someone who may have already made the choice to abort. God forgives, and we can overcome the pain and shame of that as well. There are plenty of post-abortion counseling groups available that can bring you to a place of hope and healing for the future. It's all a matter of taking the lessons that God is teaching you, and using them to turn around and bless others.

A few short months after I volunteered, the director of the HOPE Center called me into her office and asked me if I would like to share my story with others. Soon I found myself standing in front of large church groups, telling my story and speaking to other girls and women about choosing life, and becoming a mentor to countless others. God used my tests to develop my testimony, my mess to be my message. And my History was His Story…of overcoming all the odds through his grace, mercy, and never-ending love, given at those times when I knew I didn't deserve it. What an awesome, amazing God we serve!!

I understand why I chose to serve Him. But even more amazing was the fact that before all of that, before I was even in my mother's womb…He chose me.

But you are a chosen people, a royal priesthood, a holy nation, a people belonging to God, that you may declare the praises of him who called you out of darkness into his wonderful light. Once you were not a people, but now you are the people of God; once you had not received mercy, but now you have received mercy.
~1 Peter: 2:9-10

CHAPTER 17

Endings and Beginnings

SINCE THE DAYS OF ADAM AND EVE, God continues today to gives us free will to make the decisions that affect our lives, families, and futures. He has a purpose for each of us, but He will never force His way or will upon us. As shown here clearly in Deuteronomy 30:19, He clearly does give us the right to make our most difficult choices, and in the end, we must be willing to take responsibility for those choices we have made:

"This day I call heaven and earth as witnesses against you that I have set before your life and death, blessings and curses."

He doesn't force us which way to go, but with the loving guidance of a wise father who is concerned for our welfare, He gives us choices and the freedom to make the decision concerning those choices. Even more loving, He gives us a hint that will help to ensure that things go well for us in the future: *"…Now choose life, so that you and your children may live!"* (Deut 30:19)

Choose Life.

This year Gerald and I are celebrating twenty years of marriage. It has been twenty years since my call to that abortion clinic on that desperate evening, twenty years since Karen and David took in that confused and worried teenager, twenty years since I turned my heart over to Christ and made him the head over my life. The things Karen and David did for me in their obedience to God has reached and touched thousands. To this day, I do not think they are fully aware of the long-term effects that the decision they made years ago to nurture me has had on so many lives. This book will be my gift to them, in order to show them the far-reaching impact.

When you plant a seed, at first it seems small and insignificant, but the smallest seeds can grow to be huge and mighty trees bearing fruit that may feed thousands. As Christians, we are commissioned to go out and "bear fruit" from the tragedies and triumphs in our own lives. The Bible is not a book of harsh rules imposed by an evil dictator conjuring up ways to kill our fun, but a book of love stories by a Father who illustrates His unfailing adoration, and redemption of mankind. Its purpose is that we can read those tales of struggle from others who have missed the mark: such as Adam, Daniel, Joseph, David, Moses, and Paul, so that we are able to see ourselves in their struggles, and be inspired in the overcoming of them. It also helps us to see the examples set by Jesus that will teach us lessons and show us how to live and love others in our daily lives. Our story is a shared story. This life has no different challenges, just different tactics used by the enemy. The basic concept of sin is still the same: to get us to selfishly choose our will over God's. And that could be in any choice we have as humans, whether a thousand years ago or today.

"No temptation has overtaken you except such as is common to man; but God is faithful, who will not allow you to be tempted beyond what you are able, but with the temptation will also make the way of escape, that you may be able to bear it"
(1 Corinthians 10:13).

It's only when we begin to examine, admit to, and uproot the selfishness that we harbor and are willing to become totally open to where God is trying to lead us that we open ourselves up to the vast array of blessings He has waiting for us.

God once took a young girl with limited potential and turned her into a woman with unlimited possibilities, given a purpose to empower others. Did things always go great? No. In my own marriage and family life, we have had extreme challenges over the years that caused us to stumble in our faith many times. Everything was a learning experience, and since we did not have those role models in our lives, many times we learned from trial and error. The enemy sees strength in our family and has worked equally as hard through people, temptations, and adverse situations to tear apart what God means for good. Our goal is simply to keep getting back up and moving forward in the call that He has for our lives.

The lesson here is that you may be making some rather serious mistakes and have not chosen wisely in the past, but if that's the case, you are still alive and it's never too late to start from TODAY forging new paths, and making new decisions. There is always the opportunity to do things over. Repentance is not just about saying *I'm sorry*. Repentance is about changing direction, and going the opposite direction. Repentance is akin to making a virtual U-turn in the behaviors you are displaying that may separate you from God—recognizing that it's time to go the opposite way and take a different path. Yes, you may have fallen down at one point, but you don't have to stay there. God gives you a new opportunity each morning to start over.

"Great is his faithfulness; his mercies begin afresh each morning"
(Lamentations 3:23).

There is somewhere a young girl, sitting alone in a room, who is angry and confused. She is unexpectedly pregnant and not sure what to do. There is somewhere a woman wondering whether or not her volunteer work will change and affect lives, or if she can ever make a difference. There is a young man out there who wonders whether to leave, or stay with his family, and the mother of his child. There is somewhere a director of a pregnancy center looking at her budget and wondering if they should shut down, because the finances and work are overwhelming and she doesn't know if what they are doing is truly making an impact. There is a teacher who loves God and sees the rebellion in children and wonders if she can ever change things.
All of these people are here: *This is OUR story.*

As you stare at the choices that lay before you, think of my story and the countless people who don't even KNOW that what they contributed made a difference. When you think of your choices, don't just think of how YOUR life will be affected, but the thousands of lives that you have the potential to change with every decision. This goes beyond us and affects the generations that will come after us. And remember that God is there with you. He has never left or forsaken you, and if you will allow Him, He will turn things around and perform miracles you never thought possible!

In my own life, I am a pilgrim. I was able to forge new paths that changed things. We started new traditions, created new rules, and became "rebels" by making the Bible our manual.

Twenty years ago, I, like the character in the Robert Frost poem, stood at that fork in the road, wondering which path to take. To this day, I continue to thank God I was courageous enough to be able to make a decision to choose life—one that I will never regret.

> *And I...I took the one less traveled by,*
> *...And that has made all the difference.*

Epilogue

THANK YOU for reading my story. I pray that you were empowered and encouraged to do more and allow your own story to speak to others. It took me twenty years to write this book, and I didn't even know I had a story until I decided to go back to school and was forced to give an eight-minute speech in oral communications class, titled: "The single incident that made me who I am today." It took days of thinking, and finally God impressed upon me this story. For years, I knew there was something I should be writing about my life, but not sure what. For the class, I told the entire condensed version in eight minutes, and people were moved and inspired, and my teacher told me I had a BOOK in me. This lit a fire deep within, and I knew by the Spirit this was it—I had to tell this amazing story—of love, redemption, and restoration. Even twenty years later, I am still moved and awed by what God revealed to me while I was writing it. There have been many tears shed during the writing as God reminded me of His enduring and persistent love for me that over the years I had forgotten so many times. But He never let me go. He continued to show me that my story would help others, and stayed on me until I fully told it, like any good parent would do.

Since Karen and David took me in, my life has never been the same. I have had the opportunity to speak to many churches and youth groups, I have led ministry drama teams, and have written a book detailing the effects of abortion in our communities. I have developed a teen abstinence program within the pregnancy centers, and was eventually seen and invited to teach abstinence to our youth in the public schools, which I did for six years. As a family, we have taken in countless friends and family members, and become mentors to our children's friends who needed a family, sometimes having fourteen teens in our home at one time. Gerald and I have been leaders in marriage ministry and teachers in the University of the Family "Married 4 Life" classes (now called 3=1). We have developed youth programs in various states across the country and are now working with a former NBA player on a life skills program for underprivileged youth that we hope to release in late 2013.

In 2000 we started our own security company and became wealthy, but lost it in the 2007 economic crash. However, Gerald is in the process of rebuilding it, and meanwhile God has given us ministry work to focus on. I currently work with a partner on developing B.L.O.G. Online Magazine™, which currently features fifty-three writers from all over the U.S. I am also completing an exciting new workshop called The Heartwood Project™, a sixteen-hour intensive three-day workshop, which teaches and empowers women to overcome the hurts and challenges of their past by digging up the roots of the past to prevent them from affecting the next generation. Again, none of this in my own efforts, but this is all just taking the lessons God showed me and using them to empower others.

Our children also developed a love for God and now host their own Bible studies, minister to others on their college campuses, and mentor and challenge other teens to seek and maintain a walk with Christ. Our oldest son Gerald is now married with two young sons at the time of this writing. One of my greatest joys is watching him pray and read the

Bible to his wife and children each night. The choices I made are now affecting a third generation.

My daughter Ashley is a beautiful, smart, lovely young lady who has always had God moving on her life. She turns twenty years old as of this writing and was enrolled in the University of Memphis where she majored in nursing. Ashley continues to touch many lives and brings joy to all who encounter her. We feel blessed that God moved through me to give her life, and know that she has a purpose for being that will one day be revealed. The enemy tried from conception (and still continues to try) to take her out of this earth, and our continued prayers are that his plans are derailed and that God has the last word. We pray that her story will be a testimony to young girls everywhere who desire to learn to love themselves and God more deeply.

I still keep in touch with Karen and David through emails and pictures. They are still active in the ministry, and now have six children and one grandchild of their own. They are still as sweet and loving as they ever were. I miss them. After me, they took in several other teens as well. Although I have not seen them in years, my wish is to make a journey to Idaho and spend a week with them, just loving on them and showing them exactly what they meant to me. I would love most of all to introduce my children to these people who had such an impact on our lives, and changed my life in ways I can never thank them enough for. Praise God for people like them with the heart to serve and use their lives to bless others. The world needs more people like them.

If you have a heart to serve, consider contacting your local crisis pregnancy center and volunteering your time and resources for those in your community who are struggling with a decision between life and death. Your efforts can greatly make the difference in a world where human life is so devalued across the board. If you have a loving marriage and family, bless someone who didn't by prayerfully deciding to be a host family to someone who otherwise would never see this type of family and lifestyle, and that God may use you to bring them closer to the knowledge of Him. Use your story, your life, your testimony to bless others.

Don't worry about whether you made a difference to everyone you worked with. Just continue to be a light to those around you, and plant seeds, making a mark that can never be erased!

So is my word that goes out from my mouth: It will not return to me empty, but will accomplish what I desire and achieve the purpose for which I sent it.
~Isaiah 55:11

www.ingramcontent.com/pod-product-compliance
Lightning Source LLC
LaVergne TN
LVHW011420080426
835512LV00005B/181